Prayertim

By the same author

POCKET BOOK OF PRAYERS

DAILY WE TOUCH HIM
PRACTICAL RELIGIOUS EXPERIENCES

CENTERING PRAYER
RENEWING AN ANCIENT CHRISTIAN
PRAYER FORM

CENTERED LIVING
THE WAY OF CENTERING PRAYER

A PLACE APART
MONASTIC PRAYER AND PRACTICE
FOR EVERYONE

THE EUCHARIST YESTERDAY AND
TODAY

CHALLENGES IN PRAYER

BREAKING BREAD
THE TABLE TALK OF JESUS

MARY TODAY
THE CHALLENGING WOMAN

Prayertimes

MORNING
MIDDAY
EVENING

Arranged by
M. Basil Pennington, o.c.s.o.

An Image Book
Doubleday
NEW YORK   LONDON   TORONTO   SYDNEY   AUCKLAND

An Image Book
Published by Doubleday, a division of
Bantam Doubleday Dell Publishing Group, Inc.,
666 Fifth Avenue, New York, New York 10103

Image, Doubleday and the portrayal of a cross
intersecting a circle are trademarks of Doubleday, a
division of Bantam Doubleday Dell Publishing Group, Inc.

The Scriptures follow the Bible of Jerusalem except where they
have been arranged or translated by the compiler.

Library of Congress Cataloging-in-Publication Data

Pennington, M. Basil.
    Prayertimes: morning, midday, evening.

    1. Catholic Church—Prayer-books and devotions—
English.   I. Title.
BX2110.P46   1987   242'.802

Library of Congress Catalog Card Number: 87-4212
ISBN 0-385-24061-9 (pbk.)

2 4 6 8 9 7 5 3

OPM

To
all my sisters and brothers in Christ
who want to pray with Him and our Church
even while they respond to the many calls to service.
May this simple arrangement serve you.
May you find great joy in this shared prayer
that is ever old and ever new.
May you find joy and encouragement
in knowing that nuns and monks throughout the world
pray with you.

Contents

Introduction

Christianity is Judaism which has accepted the unlikely but actual Messiah, Rabbi Jesus from Nazareth. Only reluctantly did the Rabbi's followers separate themselves from their kinsfolk or accept the separation imposed upon them. They struggled for decades in indecision as to what of the Torah was still binding, as to what customs were still helpful.

Jesus had grown up practicing and faithfully following the prayer observances of God's Chosen People. His disciples continued in his ways. We find Peter and John going up to the Temple at "the hour of prayer, the ninth hour" (Acts of Apostles 3:1). As the early Christians became separated from the Synagogues and the Temple, they began their own meetings for prayer, just as they were already meeting for the Breaking of the Bread.

The Jews of Jesus' time used the same computation of time as the Romans did, day beginning at sunrise. Besides the gathering for the morning and evening sacrifice, they gathered for prayer at the third, sixth, and ninth hours—that is, midmorning (around nine A.M.), noon, and midafternoon (around three P.M.). From the Latin words for third, sixth and ninth these prayer services came to be called Terce, Sext and None. Besides these day hours of prayer, there were the watches in the night. Through the influence of monks, the more private prayers that were recited just before one retired came to be added to these as another common service: Compline. Thus the Christian community came to have these gatherings for prayer: Matins or Vigils, the watches in the night; Morning Prayer, called Lauds, which means praise, because it was primarily a prayer of praise; Terce; Sext; None; Evening Prayer, called Vespers, from the Latin word for evening; and Compline.

Of course, it was not possible for all the community to gather for all of these services; nor had it been expected among Jesus' people. There developed rather quickly communities of Christians who felt called to dedicate their lives more fully to prayer and praise, somewhat like the Levites among the Jews. These virgins and monks observed the hours of prayer quite fully. Later, bishops began to gather their clergy around them to offer the hours of prayer regularly in their principal church, the cathedral. As dioceses with many parishes developed, only certain clergy were deputed to these services at the cathedral—they were called "canons"; the rest of the clergy prayed these hours in their own parish churches with some of their flock, when possible, or on their own. This responsibility of the clergy prompted these services to be called the "office," from the Latin word for duty or responsibility.

Breviaries, small books containing the different prayers of these services, were developed for the use of these priests. The rest of the Christian community joined in this prayer according to their means and attraction. Morning and Evening Prayer —Lauds and Vespers—remained the focal points. Till this day, and perhaps more and more today, these services are coming back into the parishes, more in Europe than in the United States.

In the recent liturgical renewal, there was a recognition that priests who were leading active lives of ministry among the people could not reasonably be expected to make time for all these prayer services. So, while nuns and monks continued the traditional hours of service, some adjustments were made for those living a more engaged life in the larger community. The three day hours were combined into one. Watches in the night are not too practical for most—though our Master, even in the midst of his busy apostolic years, did watch in the night with his Father—so the service of Matins or Vigils was replaced with an "Office of Readings," emphasizing how important it is for every Christian to take time each day and let God speak to him or her through the Sacred Scriptures and through the faith of fellow Christians, especially those who were very gifted like the Fathers and Doctors of the Church.

Over the centuries, the prayer services of the Church became very complicated as generation after generation sought to enrich them by adding their own compositions. Repeatedly there were reforms or renewals, paring the services back to their primitive simplicity. In this brief breviary I seek to keep the services as simple as possible. There is some loss in this: beautiful texts, with rich variety, can inspire devotion. Yet the essential is to pray in union with the Church—the whole Church: our Head, the Lord Jesus, and all the members of today, in all parts of the world, and of yesterday, reaching back to Mary and the apostles, and even back into the Jewish community (David and all those who sang in the Temple at Jerusalem and in the synagogues), which was the Church in preparation.

Pope Paul VI noted that "the example of tradition and the interior activity of the Holy Spirit are leading modern Christians to use the Bible more and more as the basic prayer book and to draw from it genuine inspiration and splendid examples." The office or prayer book of the Church is almost wholly drawn from the older, divinely inspired prayer book of the Chosen People and the equally inspired texts that joined it to make up the Christian Bible. As we pray this prayer of the Church, the breviary or office, we pray in great part as Jesus, Mary and Joseph, Peter, Paul, and John prayed. In our oneness in the Body of Christ, members of him our head, we do in fact pray with them in that eternal "now" of God, which embraces all times and knows them to be one in him.

Some practical advice on using this Breviary or Liturgy of the Hours:

You will want to pray the Morning, Midday, and Evening Prayer each at its respective time. If you are impeded, don't try to fit them in some other time, but rather offer what impeded you as your prayer for that time. The Office of Readings can find its time whenever it is most convenient for you. Compline is meant to be prayed shortly before retiring. If you pray it regularly, you will soon be able to pray it from memory in whatever way is most appropriate for you and those with whom you pray.

The text is arranged so that you can pray the hours right through without having to move about the book. There are psalms and readings for each day of the week. The "common" office gives you the basic order; you may feel free always to use it just as it is found in the book. This may lead to a certain sense of habitual routine. This is not bad. When the text preoccupies us less, we are freer to attend to the deeper reality.

However, in order to enrich our prayer life and to move more closely with the praying Church, there are optional hymns, readings, and prayers offered for the different liturgical seasons as well as the feasts of the saints and the Blessed Virgin Mary. These are *optional*. If you do choose to use an optional hymn, reading, or prayer, this simply replaces that part from the "common" office.

Always feel free to replace any of the texts found in this book with others which are appropriate. A group using this book regularly may well want to enlarge their repertoire of hymns. You may have favorite psalms you would like to use more frequently or add on a particular day. Readings can be drawn from any part of Sacred Scripture or from other suitable books. Spontaneous prayer, coming out of the heart nourished by the psalms and readings, is certainly to be encouraged. The prayers printed in the text are only meant to foster this.

There are many ways to pray the office. We can largely seek, as the tradition often expressed it, to bring our minds and hearts into oneness with our voices, with the words we pray. We can follow the words as we pray. Or we can let a particular thought or attitude embrace us and let it remain as we go on saying the words. Another possibility is to allow the words to be but a sort of background, somewhat as we allow the "Hail Marys" of the rosary to serve us, to leave an open space to be more simply to God. Most likely, we will find ourselves employing all of these, more or less spontaneously, as we pray along. We really do not know how to pray as we ought. We begin to allow the Holy Spirit to teach us by taking up these words inspired by her. Gradually, as we move along, we open more and more to the moving of the Holy Spirit. When the drawing is there, we should not hesitate to lay aside the book and simply enter into the deeper prayer of simple presence. To facilitate this I have included in an appendix the ancient model of Centering Prayer.

M. Basil Pennington, o.c.s.o.

Saint Joseph's Abbey
Feast of the Holy Mother of God, 1987

Morning Prayer (Lauds)

Opening

V. Blessed be the name of the Lord
from this time forth and for ever more.
R. From the rising of the sun to its setting,
the name of the Lord is to be praised.
Glory be to the Father and to the Son and to the
Holy Spirit,
As it was in the beginning, is now and ever shall
be. Amen.

Hymn

Splendor of the Father's glory,
Gift of Light from Light;
Light's own Light and Fount of Light,
Daylight of each day!

Sun most true, arise!
Timeless radiance yours.

Glory of the Holy Spirit
Dawn within our souls.

Father of ageless glory,
Father of grace so strong,
Father, souls cry loud to you:
Destroy the wiles of sin.

Make our actions strong,
The fangs of envy break.
Give power to wrestle on with life,
Hard things turn to good.

Christ be our daily bread,
Faith a gladdening wine.
Make drunk our souls in joy with God's
Most pure sobriety.

Hearts be pure as dawn,
Faith be light as noon.
May mind not know the blinding dusk,
The day's whole course be joy.

Break, dawn, upon the world,
Dawn, Christ, within the soul,
Christ wholly in the Father found,
the Father in the Son.

Glory to God the Father,
To Christ, his only Son;

Glory to Spirit Paraclete
Now and beyond all time. **Amen.**

The proper hymn of the feast or season or any other hymn may be used.

Psalms
SUNDAY

Psalm 118 [117]

Alleluia!

Give thanks to Yahweh, for he is good,
    his love is everlasting!
Let the House of Israel say it,
    "His love is everlasting!"

Let the House of Aaron say it,
    "His love is everlasting!"
Let those who fear Yahweh say it,
    "His love is everlasting!"

Hard-pressed, I invoked Yahweh,
    he heard me and came to my relief.
With Yahweh on my side, I fear nothing:
    what can man do to me?
With Yahweh on my side, best help of all,
    I can triumph over my enemies.

I would rather take refuge in Yahweh
    than rely on men;
I would rather take refuge in Yahweh
    than rely on princes.

The pagans were swarming round me,
in the name of Yahweh I cut them down;
they swarmed round me closer and closer,
in the name of Yahweh I cut them down;

they swarmed round me like bees,
they blazed like a thorn-fire,
in the name of Yahweh I cut them down.

I was pressed, pressed, about to fall,
    but Yahweh came to my help;
Yahweh is my strength and my song,
    he has been my savior.

Shouts of joy and safety
    in the tents of the virtuous:
Yahweh's right hand is wrecking havoc,
    Yahweh's right hand is winning,
Yahweh's right hand is wrecking havoc!

No, I shall not die, I shall live
    to recite the deeds of Yahweh;
though Yahweh has punished me often,
    he has not abandoned me to Death.

Open the gates of virtue to me,
    I will come in and give thanks to Yahweh.
This is Yahweh's gateway,
    through which the virtuous may enter.
I thank you for having heard me,
    you have been my savior.

It was the stone rejected by the builders
that proved to be the keystone;
this is Yahweh's doing
and it is wonderful to see.
This is the day made memorable by Yahweh,
what immense joy for us!

Please, Yahweh, please save us.
Please, Yahweh, please give us prosperity.
Blessings on those who come in the name of
    Yahweh!
We bless you from the house of Yahweh.
Yahweh is God, he smiles on us.
With branches in your hands draw up in
    procession
as far as the horns of the altar,

You are my God, I give you thanks,
    I extol you, my God;
I give you thanks for having heard me,
    you have been my savior.
Give thanks to Yahweh, for he is good,
    his love is everlasting!

Praise to the Father almighty,
    to his Son, Jesus Christ, our Lord,
to their Spirit who dwells in our hearts,
    both now and forever. AMEN.

The Canticle of the Three Young Men
Daniel 3:52-57

Blest are you, O Lord, the God of our fathers,
and blest is your holy and glorious name,
    praiseworthy and exalted above all forever.

Blest are you in the temple of your holy glory,
blest are you who look into the depths from your
  throne on the cherubim,
    praiseworthy and exalted above all forever.

Blest are you in the firmament of heaven,
Bless the Lord, all you works of the Lord,
    praise and exalt him above all forever.

Angels of the Lord, bless the Lord.
You heavens, bless the Lord,
    praise and exalt him above all forever.
Bless the God of gods, all you who fear the Lord;
praise him and give him thanks,
    because his mercy endures for ever.
Praise to the Father almighty,
to his Son, Jesus Christ, our Lord,
to their Spirit who dwells in our hearts,
both now and forever. AMEN.

Psalm 150

Alleluia!

Praise God in his Temple on earth,
praise him in his temple in heaven,
praise him for his mighty achievements,
praise him for his transcendent greatness!

Praise him with blasts of the trumpet,
praise him with lyre and harp,
praise him with drums and dancing,
praise him with strings and reeds,
praise him with clashing cymbals,
praise him with clanging cymbals!
Let everything that breathes praise Yahweh!

Alleluia!

Praise to the Father almighty,
to his Son, Jesus Christ, our Lord,
to their Spirit who dwells in our hearts,
both now and forever. AMEN.

MONDAY

Psalm 5

Yahweh, let my words come to your ears,
    spare a thought for my sighs.
Listen to my cry for help,
    my King and my God!

I say this prayer to you, Yahweh,
    for at daybreak you listen to my voice;
and at dawn I hold myself in readiness for you,
    I watch for you.

You are not a God who is pleased with
  wickedness,
    you have no room for the wicked;
boasters collapse
    under your scrutiny.

You hate all evil men,
    liars you destroy;
murders and frauds
    Yahweh detests.

But I, so great is your love,
    may come to your house,
and before your holy Temple bow down
    in reverence to you.

Yahweh, lead me in the path of your
    righteousness,
        for there are men lying in wait for me;
make your way plain before me.

Not a word from their lips can be trusted,
    deep within them lies ruin,
their throats are yawning graves;
        they make their tongues so smooth!

Pronounce them guilty, God,
    Make their intrigues their own downfall!
Hound them for their countless crimes
        since they have rebelled against you.

But joy for all who take shelter in you,
    endless shouts of joy!
Since you protect them, they exult in you,
        those who love your name.

It is you who bless the virtuous man, Yahweh;
your favour is like a shield covering him.

Praise to the Father almighty,
    to his Son, Jesus Christ, our Lord,
to their Spirit who dwells in our hearts,
        both now and forever. AMEN.

A Canticle of Jeremiah
Jeremiah 31:10–14

O nations, hear the word of the Lord,
    proclaim it to the far-off coasts.

Say: "He who scattered Israel will gather him
    and guard him as a shepherd guards his
flock."

For the Lord has ransomed Jacob,
    has saved him from an overpowering hand.

They will come and shout for joy on Mount Zion,
    they will stream to the blessings of the Lord,

to corn, the new wine and the oil,
    to the flocks of sheep and the herds.

Their life will be like a watered garden.
    They will never be weary again.

Then the young girl will rejoice and will dance,
    the men, young and old, will be glad.

I will turn their mourning into joy,
    I will console them, give gladness for grief.

The priests I will again feed with plenty,
    and my people shall be filled with my
blessings.

Praise to the Father almighty,
    to his Son, Jesus Christ, our Lord,
to their Spirit who dwells in our hearts,
    both now and forever. AMEN.

Psalm 96 [95]

Sing Yahweh a new song!
Sing to Yahweh, all the earth!
Sing to Yahweh, bless his name.

Praise his salvation day after day,
tell of his glory among the nations,
tell his marvels to every people.

Yahweh is great, loud must be his praise,
he is to be feared beyond all gods.
Nothingness, all the gods of the nations.

Yahweh himself made the heavens,
in his presence are splendor and majesty,
in his sanctuary power and beauty.

Pay tribute to Yahweh, families of the peoples,
tribute to Yahweh of glory and power,
tribute to Yahweh of his name's due glory.

Bring out the offering, bear it before him,
worship Yahweh in his sacred court,
tremble before him, all the earth!

Say among the nations, "Yahweh is king!"
Firm has he made the world, and unshakable;
he will judge each nation with strict justice.

Let the heavens be glad, let the earth rejoice,
let the sea thunder and all that it holds,
let the fields exult and all that is in them,
let all the woodland trees cry out for joy,

at the presence of Yahweh, for he comes,
he comes to judge the earth,
to judge the world with justice
and the nations with his truth.

Praise to the Father almighty,
to his Son, Jesus Christ, our Lord,
to their Spirit who dwells in our hearts,
both now and forever. AMEN.

TUESDAY

Psalm 23 [22]

Yahweh is my shepherd,
  I lack nothing.

In meadows of green grass he lets me lie.
To the waters of repose he leads me;
  there he revives my soul.

He guides me by paths of virtue
  for the sake of his name.

Though I pass through a gloomy valley,
  I fear no harm;
beside me your rod and your staff
  are there, to hearten me.

You prepare a table for me
  under the eyes of my enemies;
you anoint my head with oil,
  my cup brims over.

Ah, how goodness and kindness pursue me,
  every day of my life;
my home, the house of Yahweh,
  as long as I live.

Praise to the Father almighty,
  to his Son, Jesus Christ, our Lord,

to their Spirit who dwells in our hearts,
    both now and forever. AMEN

A Canticle of Isaiah
Isaiah 42:10–16

Sing to the Lord a new song,
    his praise from the end of the earth:

Let the sea and what fills it resound,
    the coastlands, and those who dwell in them.

Let the plain and its cities cry out,
    the villages where Kedar dwells;

Let the inhabitants of Sela exult,
    and shout from the top of the mountains.

Let them give glory to the Lord,
    and utter his praise in the coastlands.

The Lord goes forth like a hero,
    like a warrior he stirs up his ardor;

He shouts out his battle cry,
    against his enemies he shows his might:

I have looked away and kept silence,
    I have said nothing, holding myself in;

But now, I cry out as a woman in labor,
  gasping and panting.

I will lay waste mountains and hills,
  all their foliage I will dry up;

I will turn the rivers into marshes;
  and the marshes I will dry up.

I will lead the blind on their journey;
  by paths unknown I will guide them.
I will turn darkness into light before them,
  and make crooked ways straight.

These things I do for them,
  and I will not forsake them.

Praise to the Father almighty,
  to his Son, Jesus Christ, our Lord,
to their Spirit who dwells in our hearts,
  both now and forever. AMEN.

Psalm 145 [144]

I sing your praises, God my King.
I bless your name forever and ever,
blessing you day after day,
and praising your name forever and ever.
Can anyone measure the magnificence
of Yahweh the great, and his inexpressible
  grandeur!

Celebrating your acts of power,
one age shall praise your doings to another.
Oh, the splendour of your glory, your renown!
I tell myself the story of your marvelous deeds.

Men will proclaim your fearful power
and I shall assert your greatness;
they will celebrate your generous kindness
and joyfully acclaim your righteousness.

He, Yahweh, is merciful, tenderhearted,
slow to anger, very loving,
and universally kind; Yahweh's tenderness
embraces all his creatures.

Yahweh, all your creatures thank you,
and your faithful bless you.
Kingly and glorious they proclaim you,
they affirm your might.

Let mankind learn your acts of power,
and the majestic glory of your sovereignty!
Your sovereignty is an eternal sovereignty,
your empire lasts from age to age.

Always true to his promises,
Yahweh shows love in all he does.
Only stumble, and Yahweh at once supports you,
if others bow you down, he will raise you up.

Patiently all creatures look to you
to feed them throughout the year;

31

quick to satisfy every need,
you feed them all with a generous hand.

Righteous in all that he does,
Yahweh acts only out of love,
standing close to all who invoke him,
close to all who invoke Yahweh faithfully.

Those who fear him need only ask to be an-
    swered;
he hears their cries for help and saves them.
Under his protection the pious are safe,
but Yahweh is destruction to the wicked.

Yahweh's praise be ever in my mouth,
and let every creature bless his holy name
        forever and ever!

Praise to the Father almighty
        to his Son, Jesus Christ, our Lord,
to their Spirit who dwells in our hearts,
        both now and forever. AMEN.

WEDNESDAY

Psalm 24 [23]

To Yahweh belong earth and all it holds,
the world and all who live in it;
he himself founded it on the ocean,
based it firmly on the nether sea.

Who has the right to climb the mountain of
    Yahweh,
who the right to stand in his holy place?
He whose hands are clean, whose heart is pure,
whose soul does not pay homage to worthless
    things
and who never swears to a lie.

The blessing of Yahweh is his,
and vindication from God his savior.
Such are the people who seek him,
who seek your presence, God of Jacob!

Gates, raise your arches,
rise, you ancient doors,
let the king of glory in!

Who is this king of glory?
Yahweh the strong, the valiant,
Yahweh valiant in battle!

Gates, raise your arches,
rise, you ancient doors,
let the king of glory in!

Who is this king of glory?
He is Yahweh Sabaoth,
King of glory, he!

Praise to the Father almighty,
    to his Son, Jesus Christ, our Lord,
to their Spirit who dwells in our hearts,
    both now and forever. AMEN.

The Canticle of Anna
1 Samuel 2:1–10

My heart exalts in the Lord,
    I find my strength in my God;

my mouth laughs at my enemies
    as I rejoice in your saving help.

There is none holy like the Lord,
there is no other save you.
    There is no Rock like our God.

The bows of the mighty are broken,
    but the weak are clothed with strength.

Those with plenty must labor for bread,
    but the hungry need work no more.

The childless wife has children now
    but the fruitful wife bears no more.

It is the Lord who gives life and death,
    he brings us to the grave and back;

it is the Lord who gives poverty and riches.
    He brings us low and raises us on high.

He lifts up the lowly from the dust,
    from the dungheap he raises the poor

to set them in the company of princes,
    to give them a glorious throne.

For the pillars of the earth are the Lord's,
    on them he set the world.

He guards the step of his faithful,
    but the wicked perish in darkness. . . .

The Most High will thunder in the heavens,
    the Lord will judge the ends of the earth.

He will give power to his king
    and exalt the might of his anointed.

Praise to the Father almighty,
    to his Son, Jesus Christ, our Lord,
to their Spirit who dwells in our hearts,
    both now and forever. AMEN.

Psalm 146 [145]

Alleluia!

Praise Yahweh, my soul!
I mean to praise Yahweh all my life,
I mean to sing to my God as long as I live.

Do not put your trust in men in power,
or in any mortal man—he cannot save,
he yields his breath and goes back to the earth he
    came from,
and on that day all his schemes perish.

Happy the man who has the God of Jacob to help
    him,
whose hope is fixed on Yahweh his God,
maker of heaven and earth,
and the sea, and all that these hold!

Yahweh, forever faithful,
gives justice to those denied it,
gives food to the hungry,
gives liberty to prisoners.

Yahweh restores sight to the blind,
Yahweh straightens the bent,
Yahweh protects the stranger,
he keeps the orphan and widow.

Yahweh loves the virtuous,
and frustrates the wicked.

Yahweh reigns forever,
your God, Zion, from age to age.

Praise to the Father almighty,
    to his Son, Jesus Christ, our Lord,
to their Spirit who dwells in our hearts,
    both now and forever. AMEN.

THURSDAY

Psalm 42 [41]

As a doe longs
    for running streams,
so longs my soul
    for you, my God.

My soul thirsts for God,
    the God of my life;
when shall I go to see
    the face of God?

I have no food but tears,
    day and night;
and all day long men say to me,
    "Where is your God?"

I remember, and my soul
    melts within me:
I am on my way to the wonderful Tent,
    to the house of God,
among cries of joy and praise
    and an exultant throng.

Why so downcast, my soul,
    why do you sigh within me?
Put your hope in God: I shall praise him yet,
    my savior, my God.

When my soul is downcast within me
    I think of you;
from the land of Jordan and of Hermon,
    of you, humble mountain!

Deep is calling to deep
    as your cataracts roar;
all your waves, your breakers,
    have rolled over me.

In the daytime may Yahweh
    command his love to come,
and by night may his song be on my lips,
    a prayer to the God of my life!

Let me say to God my Rock,
    "Why do you forget me?
Why must I walk so mournfully,
    oppressed by the enemy?"

Nearly breaking my bones
    my oppressors insult me,
as all day long they ask me,
    "Where is your God?"

Why so downcast, my soul,
    why do you sigh within me?
Put your hope in God; I shall praise him yet,
    my savior, my God.

Praise to the Father almighty,
    to his Son, Jesus Christ, our Lord,

to their Spirit who dwells in our hearts,
   both now and forever. AMEN.

A Canticle of Isaiah
Isaiah 45:15–25

Truly, God of Israel, the Savior,
you are a God who lies hidden.
   They will be put to shame and disgraced, all
   who resist you.

But Israel is saved by the Lord,
saved for evermore.
   You will never be ashamed or disgraced
   through endless ages.

For this is the word of the Lord,
the creator of heaven,
   the God who made earth and shaped it, he
   who made it firm.

He did not create it in vain,
   he made it to be lived in.

"I am the Lord, there is no other.
I have not spoken in secret, in some dark place,
   I have not said to Jacob's sons, 'Search for me
   in vain.'

"I am the Lord, I speak the truth,
   I proclaim what is right.

40

"Assemble, all of you, draw near
    you who have escaped from the nations.

"They know nothing, who carry around their
        idols made of wood
    and keep on praying to a god that cannot
        save them.

"Turn to me and be saved, all the ends of the
        earth!
    For I am God, there is no other; by myself I
        swear it.

"It is truth that goes forth from my mouth,
    a word beyond recall.

"To me every knee shall bow,
    every tongue shall swear.

"They will say, 'In the Lord alone are victory and
        power.
    And to him will come in dismay all who have
        resisted.

"Through the Lord will come victory and glory
    for all Israel's sons.'"

Praise to the Father almighty,
    to his Son, Jesus Christ, our Lord,
to their Spirit who dwells in our hearts,
    both now and forever. AMEN.

Psalm 147

Alleluia!

Praise Yahweh—it is good to sing
in honor of our God—sweet is his praise.

Yahweh, Restorer of Jerusalem!
He brought back Israel's exiles,
healing their broken hearts
and binding up their wounds.

He decides the number of the stars
and gives each of them a name;
our Lord is great, all-powerful,
of infinite understanding.

Yahweh, who lifts up the humble,
humbles the wicked to the ground.

Sing to Yahweh in gratitude,
play the lyre for our God:

who covers the heavens with clouds,
to provide the earth with rain,
to produce fresh grass on the hillsides
and the plants that are needed by man,
who gives their food to the cattle
and to the young ravens when they cry.

The strength of the war horse means nothing to
  him,

it is not infantry that interests him.
Yahweh is interested only in those who fear him,
in those who rely on his love.

Praise Yahweh, Jerusalem;
Zion, praise your God:
for strengthening the bars of your gates,
for blessing your citizens,
for granting you peace on your frontiers,
for feeding you on the finest wheat.

He gives an order;
his word flashes to earth:
to spread snow like a blanket,
to strew hoarfrost like ashes,

to drop ice like bread crumbs,
and when the cold is unbearable,
he sends his word to bring the thaw
and warm wind to melt the snow.

He reveals his word to Jacob,
his statutes and rulings to Israel:
he never does this for other nations,
he never reveals his rulings to them.

Praise to the Father almighty,
     to his Son, Jesus Christ, our Lord,
to their Spirit who dwells in our hearts,
     both now and forever. AMEN.

FRIDAY

Psalm 51 [50]
The Miserere

Have mercy on me, O God, in your goodness,
in your great tenderness wipe away my faults;
wash me clean of my guilt,
purify me from my sin.

For I am well aware of my faults,
I have my sin constantly in mind,
having sinned against none other than you,
having done what you regard as wrong.

You are just when you pass sentence on me,
blameless when you give judgment.
You know I was born guilty,
a sinner from the moment of conception.

Yet, since you love sincerity of heart,
teach me the secrets of wisdom.
Purify me with hyssop until I am clean;
wash me until I am whiter than snow.

Instill some joy and gladness into me,
let the bones you have crushed rejoice again.
Hide your face from my sins,
wipe out all my guilt.

God, create a clean heart in me,
put into me a new and constant spirit,
do not banish me from your presence,
do not deprive me of your holy spirit.

Be my savior again, renew my joy,
keep my spirit steady and willing;
and I shall teach transgressors the way to you,
and to you the sinners will return.

Save me from death, God my savior,
and my tongue will acclaim your righteousness;
Lord, open my lips,
and my mouth will speak out your praise.

Sacrifice gives you no pleasure,
were I to offer holocaust, you would not have it.
My sacrifice is this broken spirit,
you will not scorn this crushed and broken heart.

Show your favor graciously to Zion,
rebuild the walls of Jerusalem.
Then there will be proper sacrifice to please you
—holocaust and whole oblation—
and young bulls to be offered on your altar.

Praise to the Father almighty,
    to his Son, Jesus Christ, our Lord,
to their Spirit who dwells in our hearts,
    both now and forever. AMEN.

A Canticle of Ezekiel
Ezekiel 36:24–28

I will take you away from among the nations,
gather you from all the foreign lands,
>   and bring you back to your own land.

I will sprinkle clean water on you
to cleanse you from all your impurities,
>   and from all your idols I will cleanse you.

I will give you a new heart
>   and place a new spirit within you,

taking from your bodies your stony hearts
>   and giving you natural hearts.

I will put my spirit within you
and make you live by my statutes,
>   careful to observe my decrees.

You shall live in the land I gave your fathers;
you shall be my people,
>   and I will be your God.

Praise to the Father almighty,
>   to his Son, Jesus Christ, our Lord,
to their Spirit who dwells in our hearts,
>   both now and forever. AMEN.

Psalm 148

Alleluia!

Let heaven praise Yahweh:
praise him, heavenly heights,
praise him, all his angels,
praise him, all his armies!

Praise him, sun and moon,
praise him, shining stars,
praise him, highest heavens,
and waters above the heavens!

Let them all praise the name of Yahweh,
at whose command they were created;
he has fixed them in their place forever,
by an unalterable statute.

Let earth praise Yahweh;
sea monsters and all the deeps,
fire and hail, snow and mist,
gales that obey his decree,

mountains and hills,
orchards and forests,
wild animals and farm animals,
snakes and birds,

all kings on earth and nations,
princes, all rulers in the world,

young men and girls,
old people, and children too!

Let them all praise the name of Yahweh,
for his name and no other is sublime,
transcending earth and heaven in majesty,
raising the fortunes of his people,
to the praises of the devout,
of Israel, the people dear to him.

Praise to the Father almighty,
	to his Son, Jesus Christ, our Lord,
to their Spirit who dwells in our hearts,
	both now and forever. AMEN.

SATURDAY

Psalm 57 [56]

Take pity on me, God, take pity on me,
in you my soul takes shelter;
I take shelter in the shadow of your wings
until the destroying storm is over.

I call on God the Most High,
on God who has done everything for me:
to send from heaven and save me,
to check the people harrying me,
may God send his faithfulness and love.

I lie surrounded by lions
greedy for human prey,
their teeth are spears and arrows,
their tongue a sharp sword.

Rise high above the heavens, God,
  let your glory be over the earth!
They laid a net where I was walking
  when I was bowed with care;
they dug a pitfall for me
  but fell into it themselves!

My heart is ready, God,
  my heart is ready;
I mean to sing and play for you,
  awake, my muse,

awake, lyre and harp,
    I mean to awake the Dawn!

Lord, I mean to thank you among the peoples,
    to play music to you among the nations;
your love is high as heaven,
    your faithfulness as the clouds.
Rise high above the heavens, God,
    let your glory be over the earth!

Praise to the Father almighty,
    to his Son, Jesus Christ, our Lord,
to their Spirit who dwells in our hearts,
    both now and forever. AMEN.

Canticle of Judith
Judith 16:15–21

I will sing a new song to my God.
O Lord you are great and glorious,
    unsurpassable and marvelous in might;

May the whole of your creation serve you.
    For you spoke and all came into being;

created by the breath of your mouth.
    None can resist your word.

Though the heart of the mountains is shaken by
    the waters

and the rocks melt before you like wax,
>   yet you are gracious to those who revere you.

Of little worth is the fragrance of the sacrifice we
offer,
even less is the richness that is burnt in offering;
>   only the one who fears the Lord is of value.

Woe to the nations that rise against my people!
>   In the judgment the Lord of hosts will punish
>   them.

He will give their bodies to the fire and to the
worm
>   and they will bewail their fate forever.

Praise to the Father almighty,
>   to his Son, Jesus Christ, our Lord,
to their Spirit who dwells in our hearts,
>   both now and forever. AMEN.

Psalm 149

Alleluia!

Sing Yahweh a new song,
let the congregation of the faithful sing his praise!
Let Israel rejoice in his maker,
and Zion's children exult in their King;
let them dance in praise of his name,
playing to him on strings and drums!

For Yahweh has been kind to his people,
conferring victory on us who are weak;
The faithful exult in triumph,
prostrate before God they acclaim him
with panegyrics on their lips,
and a two-edged sword in their hands

to exact vengeance on the pagans,
to inflict punishment on the heathen,
to shackle their kings with chains,
and their nobles with fetters,
to execute the preordained sentence.
Thus gloriously are the faithful rewarded!

Praise to the Father almighty,
   to his Son, Jesus Christ, our Lord,
to their Spirit who dwells in our hearts,
   both now and forever. Amen.

Readings

Sunday. Praise and glory and wisdom and thanksgiving and honor and power and strength to our God for ever and ever. Amen. (Revelation 7:12)

Monday. The night is almost over, it will be daylight soon—let us give up all the things we prefer to do under cover of the dark; let us arm ourselves and appear in the light. (Romans 13:12)

Tuesday. Yahweh Sabaoth says this: Love the truth and peace! (Zechariah 8:19)

Wednesday. God is love and anyone who lives in love lives in God, and God lives in him. (1 John 4:16)

Thursday. Heal me, Yahweh, and I shall be really healed; save me, and I shall be saved, for you alone are my hope. (Jeremiah 17:14)

Friday. You should carry each other's troubles and thus fulfill the law of Christ. (Galatians 6:2)

Saturday. To the eternal King, the undying, invisible, and only God, be honor and glory for ever and ever. Amen. (1 Timothy 1:17)

R. Thanks be to God.

(Pause for silent reflection.)

The proper reading of the feast or season or any other reading may be used.

Conclusion

V. In the morning fill us with your love.
R. We shall exalt and rejoice all our days.

The Canticle of Zachary
The Benedictus
Luke 1:68-79

Blessed be the Lord, the God of Israel,
for he has visited his people, he has come to their
   rescue
and has raised up for us a power for salvation
in the house of his servant David,
even as he proclaimed,
by the mouth of his holy prophets from ancient
   times,
that he would save us from our enemies
and from the hands of all who hate us.
Thus he shows mercy to our ancestors,
thus he remembers his holy covenant;
the oath he swore
to our father Abraham
that he would grant us, free from fear,
to be delivered from the hands of our enemies,
to serve him in holiness and virtue
in his presence, all our days.
And you, little child,
you shall be called prophet of the Most High,
for you will go before the Lord

to prepare the way for him.
To give his people knowledge of salvation
through the forgiveness of their sins;
this by the tender mercy of our God
who from on high will bring the rising Sun to
    visit us,
to give light to those who live
in darkness and the shadow of death,
and to guide our feet
into the way of peace.

Praise to the Father almighty,
    to his Son, Jesus Christ, our Lord,
to their Spirit who dwells in our hearts,
    both now and forever. AMEN.

Lord, have mercy. Christ, have mercy. Lord, have
mercy.

Optional litanies: Appendix Three

Our Father, who art in heaven . . .

Let us pray.

(Pause for silent prayer.)

    O Jesus, through Mary we offer you all our
prayer, work, joys, and trials of this day, in union
with the holy Sacrifice of the Mass throughout the
world, in reparation for our sins and for the well-
being of the whole Church and the entire human
family, that our lives might be one with yours to

the glory of the Father in union with the Holy Spirit, our triune God, who is forever. AMEN.

V. Pray for us, O holy Mother of God,
R. That we may be made worthy of the promises of Christ.
V. Let us praise the Lord
R. And give him thanks.
V. May the divine assistance remain with us always
R. And with all our relatives and friends.
V. May all the departed through the mercy of God rest in peace.
R. AMEN.

The proper conclusion of the feast or season or some other prayer may be used.

Midday Prayer

Opening

V. O God, come to our assistance.
R. O Lord, make haste to help us.
Glory be to the Father and to the Son and to the
Holy Spirit,
As it was in the beginning, is now and ever shall
be. Amen.

Hymn

True God, most powerful Lord,
Ruling the changing world,
You flood the dawn with golden light,
The noonday with your fire.

Now quench the flames of strife,
And curb our harmful lusts.
Give health to flesh and bone and limb,
Give peace to mind and heart.

Grant kind Father this,
Who, with your only Son,
Reign with your Spirit, Paraclete,
All the ages through. AMEN.

*The proper hymn of the feast or season or any other hymn may
be used.*

Psalms
SUNDAY

Psalm 119 [118]

Ah, how happy those of blameless life
    who walk in the Law of Yahweh!
How happy those who respect his decrees,
    and seek him with their whole heart,
and, doing no evil,
    walk in his ways!
You yourself have made your precepts known,
    to be faithfully kept.
Oh, may my behavior be constant
    in keeping your statutes.
If I concentrate on your every commandment,
    I can never be put to shame.
I thank you from an upright heart,
    schooled in your rules of righteousness.
I mean to observe your statutes;
    never abandon me.

Praise to the Father almighty,
    to his Son, Jesus Christ, our Lord,
to their Spirit who dwells in our hearts,
    both now and forever. AMEN.

How can a youth remain pure?
    By behaving as your word prescribes.

I have sought you with all my heart,
>do not let me stray from your
>commandments.
I have treasured your promises in my heart,
>since I have no wish to sin against you.
How blessed are you, Yahweh!
>Teach me your statutes!
With my lips I have repeated them,
>all these rulings from your own mouth.
In the way of your decrees lies my joy,
>a joy beyond all wealth.
I mean to meditate on your precepts
>and to concentrate on your paths.
I find my delight in your statutes,
>I do not forget your word.

Praise to the Father almighty,
>to his Son, Jesus Christ, our Lord,
to their Spirit who dwells in our hearts,
>both now and forever. AMEN.

Be good to your servant and I shall live,
>I shall observe your word.
Open my eyes: I shall concentrate
>on the marvels of your law.
Exile though I am on earth,
>do not hide your commandments from me.
My soul is overcome
>with an incessant longing for your rulings.
You reprove the arrogant, the accursed
>who stray from your commandments.
Avert their insults and contempt from me,
>since I respect your decrees.

Though princes put me on trial,
    your servant will meditate on your statutes,
since your decrees are my delight,
    your statutes are my counselors.

Praise to the Father almighty,
    to his Son, Jesus Christ, our Lord,
to their Spirit who dwells in our hearts,
    both now and forever. AMEN.

MONDAY

Psalm 119 [118]

Down in the dust I lie prostrate:
    revive me as your word has guaranteed.
I admitted my behavior, you answered me,
    now teach me your statutes.
Explain to me how to keep your precepts,
    that I may meditate on your marvels.
I am sleepless with grief:
    raise me as your word has guaranteed.
Turn me from the path of delusion,
    grant me the grace of your Law.
I have chosen the way of fidelity,
    I have set my heart on your rulings.
I cling to your decrees:
    Yahweh, do not disappoint me.
I run the way of your commandments,
    since you have set me free.

Praise to the Father almighty,
    to his Son, Jesus Christ, our Lord,
to their Spirit who dwells in our hearts,
    both now and forever. AMEN.

Expound to me the way of your statutes, Yahweh,
    and I will always respect them.
Explain to me how to respect your Law
    and how to observe it wholeheartedly.

Guide me in the path of your commandments,
 since my delight is there.
Turn my heart to your decrees,
 and away from getting money.
Avert my eyes from lingering on inanities,
 give my life by your word.
Keep your promise to your servant,
 so that others in turn may fear you.
Avert the insults that I fear,
 in the kindness of your rulings.
Look how I yearn for your precepts:
 give me life by your righteousness.

Praise to the Father almighty,
 to his Son, Jesus Christ, our Lord,
to their Spirit who dwells in our hearts,
 both now and forever. AMEN.

For, Yahweh, visited by your love
 and saving help, as you have promised,
I can find an answer to the insults,
 since I rely on your word.
Do not deprive me of that faithful word,
 since my hope has always lain in you
 rulings.
Let me observe your Law unfailingly,
 for ever and ever.
So, having sought your precepts,
 I shall walk in all freedom.
I shall proclaim your decrees to kings
 without fear of disgrace.
Your commandments fill me with delight,
 I love them deeply.

I stretch out my hands to your beloved
     commandments,
     I meditate on your statutes.

Praise to the Father almighty,
     to his Son, Jesus Christ, our Lord,
to their Spirit who dwells in our hearts,
     both now and forever. AMEN.

TUESDAY

Psalm 119 [118]

Remember the word you pledged your servant,
    on which you have built my hope.
This has been my comfort in my suffering:
    that your promise gives me life.
Endlessly the arrogant have jeered at me,
    but I have not swerved from your Law.
Remembering your rulings in the past,
    Yahweh, I take comfort.
Fury grips me when I see the wicked
    abandoning your Law.
Where I live in exile,
    your statutes are psalms for me.
All night, Yahweh, I remember your name,
    and observe your law.
Surely it will count to my credit:
    that I respect your precepts.

Praise to the Father almighty,
    to his Son, Jesus Christ, our Lord,
to their Spirit who dwells in our hearts,
    both now and forever. AMEN.

Have I not said, Yahweh, that my task
    is to observe your words?
Wholeheartedly I now entreat you,
    take pity on me as you have promised!

After reflecting on my behavior,
    I turn my feet to your decrees.
Wasting no time, I hurry
    to observe your commandments.
Though the nooses of the wicked tighten around
    me,
    I do not forget your Law.
I get up at midnight to thank you
    for the righteousness of your rulings.
I am a friend to all who fear you,
    and observe your precepts.
Yahweh, your love fills the earth:
    teach me your statutes.

Praise to the Father almighty,
    to his Son, Jesus Christ, our Lord,
to their Spirit who dwells in our hearts,
    both now and forever. AMEN.

In accordance with your word, Yahweh,
    you have been good to your servant.
Teach me good sense and knowledge,
    for I rely on your commandments.
In earlier days I had to suffer, I used to stray,
    but now I remember your promise.
You so good and kind,
    teach me your statutes!
Though the arrogant tell foul lies about me,
    I wholeheartedly respect your precepts.
Their hearts are gross as fat,
    but my delight is in your Law.
It was good for me to have to suffer,
    the better to learn your statutes.

I put the law you have given
    before all the gold and silver in the world.

Praise to the Father almighty,
    to his Son, Jesus Christ, our Lord,
to their Spirit who dwells in our hearts,
    both now and forever. AMEN.

WEDNESDAY

Psalm 119 [118]

Yahweh, my maker, my preserver,
    explain your commandments for me to learn.
Seeing me, those who fear you will be glad,
    since I put my hope in your word.
I know that your rulings are righteous, Yahweh,
    that you make me suffer out of faithfulness.
Now, please let your love comfort me,
    as you have promised your servant.
Treat me tenderly, and I shall live,
    since your Law is my delight.
Shame seize the arrogant who defame me,
    when I meditate on your precepts.
May those who fear you rally to me,
    all those familiar with your decrees!
Blameless in your statutes be my heart:
    no such shame therefore for me!

Praise to the Father almighty,
    to his Son, Jesus Christ, our Lord,
to their Spirit who dwells in our hearts,
    both now and forever. AMEN.

Keeping my hope in your word,
    I have worn myself out waiting for you to
    save me,

and have strained my eyes waiting for your
    promise:
    when, I want to know, will you console
    me?
Though smoked as dry as a wine skin,
    I do not forget your statutes.
How much longer has your servant to live,
    when will you condemn my persecutors?
The arrogant have dug pitfalls for me
    in defiance of your Law.
Your commandments epitomize faithfulness;
    when liars hound me, you must help me.
Though these wretches have almost done me in,
    I have never abandoned your precepts.
Lovingly intervene, give me life,
    and I will observe your decrees.

Praise to the Father almighty,
    to his Son, Jesus Christ, our Lord,
to their Spirit who dwells in our hearts,
    both now and forever. AMEN.

Lasting to eternity, your word,
    Yahweh, unchanging in the heavens:
your faithfulness lasts age after age;
    you founded the earth to endure.
Creation is maintained by your rulings,
    since all things are your servants.
Had your Law not been my delight
    I should have perished in my suffering.
I shall never forget your precepts;
    by these you have kept me alive.

I am yours, save me,
    since I study your precepts.
The wicked may hope to destroy me,
    but I am scrupulous about your decrees.
I have noticed limitations to all perfection,
    but your commandment has no limits at all.

Praise to the Father almighty,
    to his Son, Jesus Christ, our Lord,
to their Spirit who dwells in our hearts,
    both now and forever. AMEN.

THURSDAY

Psalm 119 [118]

Meditating all day on your Law,
    how I have come to love it!
By your commandment, ever mine,
    how much wiser you have made me than my
        enemies!
How much subtler than my teachers,
    through my meditating on your decrees!
How much more perceptive than the elders,
    as a result of respecting your precepts.
I refrain my feet from every evil path,
    the better to observe your word.
I do not turn aside from your rulings,
    since you yourself teach me these.
Your promise, how sweet to my palate!
    Sweeter than honey to my mouth!
Your precepts endow me with perception;
    I hate all deceptive paths.

Praise to the Father almighty,
    to his Son, Jesus Christ, our Lord,
to their Spirit who dwells in our hearts,
    both now and forever. AMEN.

Now your word is a lamp to my feet,
    a light on my path.
I have sworn to observe, I shall maintain,
    your righteous rulings.

Yahweh, though my suffering is acute,
    revive me as your word has guaranteed.
Yahweh, accept the homage that I offer,
    teach me your rulings.
I would lay down my life at any moment,
    I have never yet forgotten your Law.
The wicked have tried to trap me,
    but I have never yet veered from your
        precepts.
Your decrees are my eternal heritage,
    they are the joy of my heart.
I devote myself to obeying your statutes—
    compensation enough forever!

Praise to the Father almighty,
    to his Son, Jesus Christ, our Lord,
to their Spirit who dwells in our hearts,
    both now and forever. AMEN.

Odious, those whose allegiance is divided;
    I love your Law!
You, my refuge and shield,
    I put my hope in your word.
Away from me you wicked people!
    I will respect the commandments of my God.
Support me as you have promised, and I shall
        live,
    do not disappoint me of my hope.
Uphold me, and I shall be safe
    with your statutes constantly before my eyes.
You spurn all who stray from your statutes,
    their notions being delusion.

You scour the wicked off the earth like rust;
    that is why I love your decrees.
My whole being trembles before you,
    your rulings fill me with fear.

Praise to the Father almighty,
    to his Son, Jesus Christ, our Lord,
to their Spirit who dwells in our hearts,
    both now and forever. Amen.

FRIDAY

Psalm 119 [118]

Persevering in justice and virtue,
>must I now be abandoned to my oppressors?
Guarantor of your servant's well-being,
>forbid the arrogant to oppress me!
My eyes are worn out looking for your saving
help,
>for your promise of righteousness to come.
Treat your servant lovingly,
>teach me your statutes.
I am your servant; if you will explain,
>I shall embrace your decrees.
Yahweh, now is the time to act,
>your Law is being broken.
Yes, I love your commandments,
>more than gold, than purest gold.
Yes, I rule myself by all your precepts;
>I hate all deceptive paths.

Praise to the Father almighty,
>to his Son, Jesus Christ, our Lord,
to their Spirit who dwells in our hearts,
>both now and forever. AMEN.

Your decrees are so wonderful
>my soul cannot but respect them.
As your word unfolds, it gives light,
>and the simple understand.

I open my mouth, panting
     eagerly for your commandments.
Turn to me please, pity me,
     as you should those who love your name.
Direct my steps as you have promised,
     let evil win no power over me.
Rescue me from human oppression;
     I will observe your precepts.
Treat your servant kindly,
     teach me your statutes.
My eyes stream with tears,
     because others disregard your Law.

Praise to the Father almighty,
     to his Son, Jesus Christ, our Lord,
to their Spirit who dwells in our hearts,
     both now and forever. AMEN.

Righteous, indeed, Yahweh!
     And all your rulings correct!
The decrees you impose, how righteous,
     how absolutely faithful!
Zeal for your house devours me,
     since my oppressors forget your word.
But your promise is well tested,
     and your servant holds it dear.
Puny and despised as I am,
     I do not forget your precepts.
Your righteousness is eternal righteousness,
     your Law holds true forever.
Though distress and anguish grip me,
     your commandments are my delight.

Eternally righteous, your decrees—
   explain them to me, and I shall live.

Praise to the Father almighty,
   to his Son, Jesus Christ, our Lord,
to their Spirit who dwells in our hearts,
   both now and forever. AMEN.

SATURDAY

Psalm 119 [118]

Sincere, my call—Yahweh, answer me!
  I will respect your statutes.
I invoke you, save me,
  I will observe your decrees.
I am up before dawn to call for help,
  I put my hope in your word.
I lie awake throughout the night,
  to meditate on your promise.
In your love, Yahweh, listen to my voice,
  let your rulings give me life.
My cruel persecutors are closing in,
  how remote they are from your Law!
But, Yahweh, you are close still
  and all your commandments are true.
Long have I known that your decrees
  were founded to last forever.

Praise to the Father almighty,
  to his Son, Jesus Christ, our Lord,
to their Spirit who dwells in our hearts,
  both now and forever. AMEN.

Take note of my suffering and rescue me,
  for I do not forget your law.
Take up my cause, defend me,
  give me life as you have promised.

77

You will never save the wicked,
    if they do not study your statutes,
but many are your mercies to me, Yahweh,
    by your rulings give me life.
Many hound me and oppress me,
    but I do not swerve from your decrees.
The sight of these renegades disgusts me,
    they do not observe your promise;
but, Yahweh, see how I love your precepts,
    and lovingly give me life.
Faithfulness is the essence of your word,
    your righteous rulings hold good for ever.

Praise to the Father almighty,
    to his Son, Jesus Christ, our Lord,
to their Spirit who dwells in our hearts,
    both now and forever. AMEN.

Unjustifiably though princes hound me,
    your word is what fills me with dread.
I rejoice in your promise,
    like someone on finding a vast treasure.
I hate, I detest delusion;
    your Law is what I love.
Seven times daily I praise you
    for your righteous rulings.
Universal peace for those who love your Law,
    no stumbling blocks for them.
Waiting for you, Yahweh, my savior,
    I fulfill your commandments.
My soul observes your decrees,
    these I wholly love.

I observe your precepts, your decrees,
    you know how I keep to your paths.

Praise to the Father almighty,
    to his Son, Jesus Christ, our Lord,
to their Spirit who dwells in our hearts,
    both now and forever. AMEN.

Readings

Sunday. God's commandment is this: we are to believe in the name of his Son, Jesus Christ, and are to love one another as he commanded us. Those who keep his commandments remain in him and he is them. And this is how we know that he remains in us: from the Spirit that he gave us. (1 John 3:23–24)

Monday. You did not receive a spirit of slavery leading you back into fear, but a spirit of adoption through which we cry out, "Abba!" (that is, "Father"). The Spirit himself gives witness with our spirit that we are children of God. (Romans 8:15–16)

Tuesday. Now there are varieties of gifts, but the same Spirit; and there are varieties of service, but the same Lord; and there are varieties of working, but it is the same God who inspires them all in everyone. To each is given the manifestation of the Spirit for the common good. (1 Corinthians 12:4–7)

Wednesday. Do nothing to sadden the Holy Spirit with whom you are sealed against the day of redemption. Get rid of all bitterness, all passion and anger, harsh words, slander, and malice of every kind. In place of these, be kind to one another, compassionate, and mutually forgiving, just as God has forgiven you in Christ. (Ephesians 4:30–32)

Thursday. Your love must be sincere. Detest what is evil, cling to what is good. Love one another with the affection of brothers and sisters. Anticipate each other in showing respect. Do not grow slack but be fervent in spirit; he whom you serve is the Lord. Rejoice in hope, be patient under trial, persevere in prayer. Look on the needs of the saints as your own; be generous in offering hospitality. (Romans 12:9–13)

Friday. The Lord is the Spirit, and where the Spirit of the Lord is there is freedom. All of us, gazing on the Lord's glory with unveiled faces, are being transformed from glory to glory into his very image by the Lord who is the Spirit. (2 Corinthians 3:17–18)

Saturday. I kneel before the Father from whom every family in heaven and on earth takes its name; and I pray that he will bestow on you gifts in keeping with the riches of his glory. May he strengthen you inwardly through the working of his Spirit. May Christ dwell in your hearts through faith, and may charity be the root and foundation of your life. Thus you will be able to grasp fully, with all the holy ones, the breadth and length and height and depth of Christ's love, and experience this love which surpasses all knowledge, so that you may attain to the fullness of God himself. (Ephesians 3:14–19)

R. Thanks be to God.

(Pause for silent reflection.)

The proper reading of the feast or season or any other reading may be used.

Conclusion

V. Send forth your Spirit, and we shall be recreated.

R. And you shall renew the face of the earth.

Lord, have mercy. Christ, have mercy. Lord, have mercy.

Optional litanies: Appendix Three

Our Father, who art in heaven. . . .

Let us pray.

(Pause for silent prayer.)

Father, open our eyes to your mercy. Awaken our hearts with your love. Give us the courage and strength to live this day for your glory and for the good of all our sisters and brothers, putting aside all selfish vanity. Keep us mindful of your helping presence. Through faith in your forgiveness may we forgive even as we have been forgiven, love as we have been loved, and live as you give us to live. We ask this through our Lord, Jesus, in the Holy Spirit. AMEN.

V. Pray for us, O holy Mother of God,
R. that we may be made worthy of the promises of Christ.
V. Let us praise the Lord
R. and give him thanks.
V. May the divine assistance remain with us always
R. and with all our relatives and friends.
V. May all the departed through the mercy of God rest in peace.
R. AMEN.

The proper conclusion of the feast or season or any other prayer may be used.

Evening Prayer (Vespers)

Opening

V. Let my evening prayer ascend before you, O Lord.

R. And let your loving kindness descend upon us.
Glory be to the Father and to the Son and to the Holy Spirit,
As it was in the beginning, is now and ever shall be. AMEN.

Hymn

Creator God of all,
You guide the coursing stars.
You clothe the day with light and beauty,
Grace the night with sleep.

May that sleep restore
Tired limbs for work again.
Refresh the jaded mind for thought,
Resolve our daily grief.

With grateful hymns and prayer
We keep our morning vows.
Help us now that weary day
Dies in the arms of night.

To you the heart will sing,
Ringing voice will praise you.
To you the purest love will cling,
Peaceful mind adore you.

When no trace of day
Lingers in the night,
May nighttime shine with brightest faith,
And faith be free from darkness.

May spirit never sleep,
But guilt be always sleeping.
While faith, refreshment of the pure,
Rob sleep of all its danger.

Freed from deceitful sense,
May heart's deep dream be you.
May not the wiles of envious foe
With fear disturb our sleep.

Christ and the Father hear,
And you their Holy Spirit,
Three, yet One in boundless power,
Enfold us in your mercy. AMEN.

Psalms
SUNDAY

Psalm 110 [109]

Yahweh's oracle to you, my Lord, "Sit at my right
   hand
and I will make my enemies a footstool for you."

Yahweh will force all your enemies
under the sway of your scepter in Zion.

Royal dignity was yours from the day you were
   born
     on the holy mountains.
Royal from the womb, from your earliest days.

Yahweh has sworn an oath which he will never
   retract
"You are a priest of the order of Melchizedeck,
   and forever."

The Lord is at your right hand.
When he grows angry he shatters kings,
he gives the nations their deserts,
smashing their skulls he heaps the wide world
   with corpses.
Drinking from the stream as he goes
he can hold his head high in victory.

Praise to the Father almighty,
    to his Son, Jesus Christ, our Lord,
to their Spirit who dwells in our hearts,
    both now and forever. AMEN.

Psalm 111 [110]

Alleluia!

I give thanks to Yahweh with all my heart
where the virtuous meet and the people assemble.

The works of Yahweh are sublime
those who delight in them are right to fix their
    eyes on them.

The work that he does is full of glory and
    majesty
and his righteousness can never change.

He allows us to commemorate his marvels.
Yahweh is merciful and tender hearted.

He provides food for those who fear him;
he never forgets his covenant.

He reminds his people of the power he wields,
by giving them the inheritance of the nations.

All that he does is done in faithfulness and
    justice,
in all ways his precepts are dependable.

88

Ordained to last for ever and ever,
framed in faithfulness and integrity.

Quickly he comes to his peoples' rescue,
imposing his covenant once and for all;
so holy his name, commanding our dread.

The fear of Yahweh is the beginning of wisdom,
they have sound sense who practice it.
His praise will be sung forever.

Praise to the Father almighty,
    to his Son, Jesus Christ, our Lord,
to their Spirit who dwells in our hearts,
    both now and forever. AMEN.

Canticle
Revelation 19:1–7

Salvation and glory and power belong to our God;
    his judgments are just and true.

Praise our God, all you his servants,
    you who fear him, small and great.

The Lord our God, the Almighty, reigns;
    rejoice and exult and give him glory.

The marriage of the Lamb has come,
    and his bride has prepared herself.

She has been given a royal robe to wear,
     of finest linen.

Give praise to the Father almighty,
     to his Son, Jesus Christ, our Lord,
to the Spirit who dwells in our hearts,
     both now and forever. AMEN.

MONDAY

Psalm 112 [111]

Alleluia!

Happy the man who fears Yahweh
by joyfully keeping his commandment!

Children of such a man will be powers on the
   earth
Descendants of the upright will ever be blessed.

There will be riches and wealth for his family
and his righteousness can never be changed.

For the upright he shines like a lamp,
he is merciful, tenderhearted, virtuous.

Interest is not charged by this good man,
he is honest in all his dealings.

Kept safe by virtue, he is ever steadfast,
and leaves an imperishable memory behind him;

With constant heart and confidence in Yahweh,
he never need fear bad news.

Steadfast and hearty, he overcomes his fears:
in the end he will triumph over his enemies.

Quick to be generous, he gives to the poor,
his righteousness can never change,

Men such as this will always be honored,
though this fills the wicked with fury,
until grinding their teeth they waste away,
vanishing like their vain hopes.

Praise to the Father almighty,
    to his Son, Jesus Christ, our Lord,
to their Spirit who dwells in our hearts,
    both now and forever. AMEN.

Psalm 113 [112]

Alleluia!

You servants of Yahweh, praise,
praise the name of Yahweh!
Blessed be the name of Yahweh,
hence forth and forever more!
From east to west,
praised be the name of Yahweh!

High above all nations Yahweh!
His glory transcends the heavens!
Who is like our God?—
He is so high he needs to stoop
to see the sky and the earth.

He raises the poor from the dust;
he lifts the needy from the dung hill

to give them a place with princes,
the princes of his people.

He enthrones the barren woman in her house
by making her the happy mother of sons.

Praise to the Father almighty,
   to his Son, Jesus Christ, our Lord,
to their Spirit who dwells in our hearts,
   both now and forever. AMEN.

Canticle
Ephesians 1:3–10

Praised be the God and Father
   of our Lord Jesus Christ.

In Christ he has bestowed on us
   every spiritual blessing in the heavens.

In him God chose us before the world began,
   to be holy and blameless in his presence.

He predestined us through Jesus Christ to be his
   adopted sons;
      such was his will and good pleasure,

that all might praise his glorious favor,
   bestowed on us in his beloved Son.

In him and through his blood, we have been
   redeemed,
      and our sins have been forgiven.

Such is the abundant goodness of God
      that he has lavished upon us.

He has given us wisdom to see fully the mystery,
      the plan he was pleased to decree.

The plan to be revealed in the fullness of time:
      all heaven and earth brought together in unity
         under the headship of Christ.

Give praise to the Father almighty,
      to his Son, Jesus Christ, our Lord,
to the Spirit who dwells in our hearts,
      both now and forever. AMEN.

TUESDAY

Psalm 24 [23]

To Yahweh belongs the earth and all it holds,
the world and all who live in it;
he himself founded it on the ocean,
based on the nether sea.

Who has the right to climb the mountain of
    Yahweh,
who has the right to stand in his holy place?
He whose hands are clean, whose heart is pure,
whose soul does not pay homage to worthless
    things,
and who never swears to a lie.

The blessing of Yahweh is his,
and vindication from God his savior.
Such are the people who seek him,
who seek your presence, God of Jacob!

Gates, raise your arches,
rise, you ancient doors,
let the King of Glory in!

Who is the King of Glory?
Yahweh, the strong, the valiant,
Yahweh, the valiant in battle!

Gates, raise your arches,
rise, you ancient doors,
let he King of Glory in!

Who is the King of Glory?
He is Yahweh Sabaoth,
King of Glory, he!

Praise to the Father almighty,
    to his Son, Jesus Christ, our Lord,
to their Spirit who dwells in our hearts,
    both now and forever. AMEN.

Psalm 65 [64]

Praise is rightfully yours,
    God in Zion.
Vows to you must be fulfilled
    for you answer prayer.

Our hearts must come to you
    with all their sins;
Though our faults overpower us,
    you blot them out.

Happy the man you choose, whom you invite
    to live in your courts,
Filled with the good things of your house
    of your holy temple.

Your righteousness repays us with marvels,
    God our savior,

hope of all the ends of the earth
        and the distant islands.

Your strength holds the mountains up,
        such is the power that wraps you;
you calm the clamor of the ocean,
        the clamor of its waves.

The nations are in uproar, in panic,
        those who live at the ends of the world,
as your miracles bring shouts of joy
        to the callers of morning and evening.

You visit the earth and water it,
        you laid it with riches;
God's rivers brim with water
        to provide their grain.

        This is how you provide it:
by drenching its furrows, by leveling its ridges,
by softening it with showers, by blessing the first
    fruits,
you crown the year with your bounty,
abundance flows wherever you pass;
the desert pastures overflow,
the hillsides are wrapped in joy,
the meadows are dressed in flocks,
the valleys are clothed in wheat,
what shouts of joy, what singing!

Praise to the Father almighty,
        to his Son, Jesus Christ, our Lord,

to their Spirit who dwells in our hearts,
  both now and forever. AMEN.

Canticle
Revelation 11:17–18; 12:10–12

We praise you, O Lord God Almighty,
  who is, who was, and who will be.

You have taken up your great power;
  you have begun your reign.

The nations raged in anger,
but then came the wrath of your day,
  the moment to judge the dead.

The time to reward your servants, the prophets,
and the holy ones who revere you,
  the great and small alike.

Now have come power and salvation,
  the reign of our God, and the rule of his
Anointed One.

Cast down is the accuser of our dear ones,
  who night and day accused them before our
God.

By the blood of the Lamb they conquered him,
  by the word and the witness they gave.

Love for life did not keep them from dying:
    so rejoice, you heavens and all who dwell
  there.

Give praise to the Father almighty,
    to his Son, Jesus Christ, our Lord,
to the Spirit who dwells in our hearts,
    both now and forever. AMEN.

WEDNESDAY

Psalm 27 [27]

Yahweh is my light and my salvation,
    whom need I fear?
Yahweh is my fortress and my life,
    of whom should I be afraid?

When evil men advance against me,
    to devour my flesh,
they my opponents, my enemies,
    are the ones who stumble and fall.

Though an army pitch camp against me,
    my heart would not fear;
though war were waged against me,
    my trust would still be firm.

One thing I ask of Yahweh,
    one thing I seek:
to live in the house of Yahweh
    all the days of my life,
to enjoy the sweetness of Yahweh,
    to consult him in his temple.

For he shelters me under his awning
    in times of trouble;
he hides me deep in his tent,
    sets me high on a rock.

And now my head is held high
    over the enemies who surround me.
In his tent I will offer
    exultant sacrifice.

I will sing! I will play for Yahweh!

Yahweh, hear my voice as I cry!
    Pity me! Answer me!
My heart has said of you,
    'Seek his face.'
Yahweh, I do seek your face;
    do not hide your face from me.

Do not repulse your servant in anger;
    You are my help.
Never leave me, never desert me,
    God, my savior!
If my father and mother desert me,
    Yahweh will care for me still.

Yahweh, teach me your way,
lead me in the path of integrity
    because of my enemies;
do not abandon me to the will of my foes—
false witnesses have risen against me,
    and breathe out violence.

This I believe: I shall see the goodness of Yahweh,
    in the land of the living.
Put your hope in Yahweh, be strong, let your
  heart be bold,
    put your hope in Yahweh.

Praise to the Father almighty,
    to his Son, Jesus Christ, our Lord,
to their Spirit who dwells in our hearts,
    both now and forever. AMEN.

Psalm 131 [130]

Yahweh, my heart has no lofty ambitions,
    my eyes do not look too high,
I am not concerned with great affairs,
    or marvels beyond my scope.
Enough for me to keep my soul tranquil and
    quiet,
    like a child in its mother's arms,
as content as a child that has been weaned.

Israel, rely on Yahweh,
    now and for always!

Praise to the Father almighty,
    to his Son, Jesus Christ, our Lord,
to their Spirit who dwells in our hearts,
    both now and forever. AMEN.

Canticle
Colossians 1:12–20

We give thanks to the Father for having made us
    worthy
    to share the lot of the saints in light.

102

He rescued us from the power of darkness,
and brought us into the kingdom of his
beloved Son.

In him we have redemption,
the forgiveness of sins.

He is the image of the unseen God,
the first-born of all creatures.

In him were all things created
in the heavens and on the earth.

Things visible and things unseen,
Thrones and Dominations, Principalities and
Powers.

All things were created through him,
and all were created for him.

He exists before all other beings,
and in him all things hold together.

It is he who is the head of the body, the Church,
he who is the Beginning.

The first-born from among the dead,
so that in all things the primacy is his.

God was pleased to make all fullness dwell in
him,
and through him, to reconcile everything in
himself.

Making peace through the blood of his cross,
both on earth and in the heavens.

Give praise to the Father almighty,
to his Son, Jesus Christ, our Lord,
to the Spirit who dwells in our hearts,
both now and forever. AMEN.

THURSDAY

Psalm 66 [65]

Acclaim God, all the earth,
play music to the glory of his name,
glorify him with your praises,
say to God, "What dread you inspire!"

Your achievements are the measure of your
    power.
Your enemies cringe in your presence;
all the earth bows down to you,
playing music for you, playing in honor of your
    name.

Come and see what marvels God has done,
so much to be feared for his deeds among
    mankind:
he turned the sea into dry land,
they crossed the river on foot.

So let us rejoice in him,
who rules forever by his power:
his eyes keep watch on the nations,
let no rebel raise his head!

You nations, bless our God,
and make his praise resound,
who brings our soul to life,
and keeps our feet from faltering.

You tested us, God,
you refined us like silver,
you let us fall into the net,
you laid heavy burdens on our backs,
you let people drive over our heads;
but now the ordeal by fire and water is over,
and you allow us once more to draw breath.

I bring holocausts to your house,
I bring them to fulfill those vows
that rose to my lips,
those vows I spoke when in trouble.

I offer you fat holocausts
and the smoke of burning rams.
I offer you bullocks and he-goats.

Come and listen, all you who fear God,
while I tell you what he has done for me:
when I uttered my cry to him
and high praise was on my tongue,
had I been guilty in my heart,
the Lord would never have heard me.
But God not only heard me,
he listened to my prayer.

    Blessed be God,
who neither ignored my prayer
nor deprived me of his love.

Praise to the Father almighty,
    to his Son, Jesus Christ, our Lord,

to their Spirit who dwells in our hearts,
    both now and forever. AMEN.

Psalm 138 [137]

I thank you, Yahweh, with all my heart
because you have heard what I said.
In the presence of the angels I play for you
and bow down toward your holy temple.

I give thanks to your name, for your love and
    faithfulness;
your promise is ever even greater than your fame.
The day I called for help you heard me,
and you increased my strength.

Yahweh, all kings on earth give thanks to you,
for they have heard your promises;
they celebrate Yahweh's actions:
Great is the glory of Yahweh!

From far above, Yahweh sees the humble,
from far away he marks down the arrogant.

I live surrounded by trouble,
you keep me alive—to my enemies' fury!
You stretch your hand out and save me,
your right hand will do everything for me.
Yahweh, your love is everlasting,
do not abandon us whom you have made.

Praise to the Father almighty,
    to his Son, Jesus Christ, our Lord,
to their Spirit who dwells in our hearts,
    both now and forever. AMEN.

Canticle
Revelation 15:3–4

Mighty and wonderful are your works,
    O Lord, Almighty God.

Just and true are all your ways,
    O King of the Ages.

Who would not give you praise, O Lord,
    and glorify your name?

For you alone are the Holy One:
    your marvels are clearly seen.

So shall all the nations come forth
    to worship in your presence.

Give praise to the Father almighty,
    to his Son, Jesus Christ, our Lord,
to the Spirit who dwells in our hearts,
    both now and forever. AMEN.

FRIDAY

Psalm 22 [21]

My God, my God, why have you deserted me?
How far from saving me, the words I groan.
I call all day, my God, but you never answer,
all night long I call and cannot rest.
Yet, Holy One, you
who make your home in the praises of Israel,
in you our fathers put their trust,
they trusted and you rescued them;
they called to you for help and they were saved;
they never trusted you in vain.

Yet here am I, now more worm than man,
scorn of mankind, jest of the people,
all who see me jeer at me,
they toss their heads and sneer,
"He relied on Yahweh, let Yahweh save him!
If Yahweh is his friend, let him rescue him!"

Yet you drew me out from the womb,
you entrusted me to my mother's breasts;
placed on your lap from my birth,
from my mother's womb you have been my God.
Do not stand aside: trouble is near,
I have no one to help me!

A herd of bulls surrounds me,
strong bulls of Bashan close in on me;

their jaws are agape for me,
like lions tearing and roaring.

I am like water draining away,
my bones are all disjointed,
my heart is like wax,
melting inside me;
my palate is drier than a potsherd,
and my tongue is stuck to my jaw.

A pack of dogs surround me,
a gang of villains close me in;
they tie me hand and foot
and leave me lying in the dust of death.

I can count every one of my bones,
and there they glare at me gloating;
they divide my garments among them
and cast lots for my clothes.

Do not stand aside, Yahweh.
O my strength come quickly to my help;
rescue my soul from the sword,
my dear life from the paw of the dog.
Save me from the lion's mouth,
my poor soul from the wild bulls' horns!

Then I shall proclaim your name to my brothers,
praise you in full assembly;
you who fear Yahweh, praise him!
Entire race of Jacob, glorify him!
Entire race of Israel, revere him!

For he has not despised
or disdained the poor man in his poverty,
has not hidden his face from him
but has answered him when he called.

You are the theme of my praise in the Great
  Assembly.
I perform my vows in the presence of those who
  fear him.
The poor will receive as much as they want to
  eat.
Those who seek Yahweh will praise him.
Long life to their hearts!

The whole earth from end to end will remember
  and come back to Yahweh;
all the families of the nations will bow down
  before him.
For Yahweh reigns, the ruler of nations!
Before him all the prosperous of the earth will
  bow down,
before him will bow down all who go down to
  the dust.
And my soul will love him, my children will serve
  him;
men will proclaim the Lord to generations still to
  come,
his righteousness to a people yet unborn. All this
  he has done.

Praise to the Father almighty,
    to his Son, Jesus Christ, our Lord,

to their Spirit who dwells in our hearts,
both now and forever. AMEN.

Psalm 130 [129]
The De profundis

From the depths I call to you, Yahweh,
Lord, listen to my cry for help!
Listen compassionately
to my pleading!

If you never overlooked our sins, Yahweh,
Lord, could anyone survive?
But you do forgive us;
and for that we revere you.

I wait for Yahweh, my soul waits for him,
I rely on his promise,
my soul relies on the Lord
more than a watchman on the coming of
dawn.

Let Israel rely on Yahweh
as much as the watchman on the dawn!
For it is with Yahweh that mercy is to be found,
and a generous redemption;
it is he who redeems Israel
from all their sins.

Give praise to the Father almighty,
to his Son, Jesus Christ, our Lord,

to the Spirit who dwells in our hearts,
	both now and forever. Amen.

Canticle
Philippians 2:6–1

Although he was in the form of God
he did not consider that he should cling
	to equality with God.

Rather did he empty himself
taking on the form of a slave,
	being born in the likeness of all men.

In outward form he was found as a man,
thus he humbled himself, obedient unto death,
	death upon a cross.

Because of this, God highly exalted him
and bestowed on him the name
	above every other name.

So that at the name of Jesus
every knee should bend,
	in the heavens, on the earth, and in the world
below.

And every tongue proclaim
to the glory of God the Father
	that Jesus Christ is Lord.

Give praise to the Father almighty,
    to his Son, Jesus Christ, our Lord,
to the Spirit who dwells in our hearts,
    both now and forever. AMEN.

SATURDAY

Psalm 133 [132]

How good, how delightful it is
    for all to live together like brothers;

fine as oil on the head,
    running down the beard,
running down Aaron's beard,
    to the collar of his robes;

copious as a Hermon dew
    falling on the heights of Zion,
where Yahweh confers his blessing,
    everlasting life.

Give praise to the Father almighty,
    to his Son, Jesus Christ, the Lord,
to the Spirit who dwells in our hearts,
    both now and forever. Amen.

Psalm 142 [141]

To Yahweh, my cry! I plead.
To Yahweh, my cry! I entreat.
I pour out my supplications,
I unfold my troubles;
my spirit fails me,
but you, you know my path.

On the path I follow
they have concealed a trap.
Look on my right and see,
there is no one to befriend me,
All help is denied me.
No one cares about me.

I invoke you, Yahweh,
I affirm that you are my refuge,
my heritage in the land of the living.
Listen to my cries for help,
I can hardly be crushed lower.

Rescue me from persecutors
stronger than I am!
Free me from this imprisonment
and I will thank your name once more
in the assembly of the virtuous
for the goodness you show me.

Praise to the Father almighty,
    to his Son, Jesus Christ, our Lord,
to their Spirit who dwells in our hearts,
    both now and forever. AMEN.

Canticle
Revelation 4:11; 5:9, 10, 12

Worthy are you, O Lord our God,
  to receive glory and honor and power,
for you created all things,
  and by your will they were made and live.

Worthy are you, O Lord,
  to take the scroll and to open its seals,
for you were slain
and by your blood you ransomed men for God
  from every tribe and tongue and nation.

You have made us a kingdom and priests to our
  God,
  and we shall reign upon the earth.

Worthy is the Lamb who was slain,
  to receive wealth and power,
and wisdom and might,
  and honor and glory and blessing.

Give praise to the Father almighty,
  to his Son, Jesus Christ, our Lord,
to the Spirit who dwells in our hearts,
  both now and forever. AMEN.

Readings

Sunday. In the beginning was the Word: the Word was with God and the Word was God. He was with God in the beginning. The Word was made flesh, he lived among us, and we saw his glory, the glory that is his as the only Son of the Father, full of grace and truth. (John 1:1 and 14)

Monday. I tell you solemnly, unless one is born through water and the Spirit, that one cannot enter the kingdom of God: what is born of the flesh is flesh; what is born of the Spirit is spirit. (John 3:5)

Tuesday. The Advocate, the Holy Spirit, whom the Father will send in my name, will teach you everything and remind you of all I have said to you. (John 14:26)

Wednesday. I am the bread of life. The one who comes to me will never be hungry; the one who believes in me will never thirst. (John 6:35)

Thursday. I tell you most solemnly, if you do not eat the flesh of the Son of Man and drink his blood, you will not have life in you. Anyone who does eat my flesh and drink my blood has eternal life and I shall raise that one up on the last day. (John 6:53–54)

Friday. I tell you most solemnly, unless a wheat grain falls on the ground and dies, it remains only a single grain; but if it dies, it yields a rich harvest. Anyone who loves his life loses it; anyone

who hates his life in this world will keep it for
the eternal life. (John 12:23–25)

Saturday. I am the true vine and my Father is the
vinedresser. Every branch in me that bears no
fruit he cuts away, and every branch that does
bear fruit he prunes to make it bear even more.
You are pruned already, by means of the word
that I have spoken to you. Make your home in
me, as I make mine in you. (John 15:1–3)

R. Thanks be to God.

(Pause for silent reflection.)

*The proper reading of the feast or season or any other suitable
reading may be used.*

Conclusion

V. Lord, let my prayer come before you,
R. like incense in your sight.

The Canticle of Mary
The Magnificat
Luke 1:46–55

My soul proclaims the greatness of the Lord
and my spirit exalts in God, my savior;
because he has looked upon his lowly handmaid.

Yes, from this day forward
    all generations will call me blessed,
for the Almighty has done great things for me.
Holy is his name,
and his mercy reaches from age to age for those
  who fear him.
He has shown the power of his arm,
he has routed the proud of heart.
He has pulled down princes from their thrones
    and exalted the lowly.
The hungry he has filled with good things,
    the rich sent empty away.
He has come to the help of Israel his servant,
    mindful of his mercy
—according to the promise he made to our
  ancestors—
of his mercy to Abraham and to his descendants
  forever.

Give praise to the Father almighty,
    to his Son, Jesus Christ, our Lord,
to the Spirit who dwells in our hearts,
    both now and forever. AMEN.

Lord, have mercy. Christ, have mercy. Lord, have
mercy.

Optional litanies: Appendix Three

Our Father, who art in heaven . . .

Let us pray.

(Pause for silent prayer.)

O Almighty God, I come before you to thank you with all my heart for all the favors you have bestowed upon me this day, for my food and drink, my health, and all the powers of my body and soul. I thank you for all your inspirations, for your care and protection, and for all those other mercies of which I am not aware. I thank you for them all, heavenly Father, through Jesus Christ our Lord. Amen.

V. Pray for us, O holy Mother of God,
R. That we may be made worthy of the promises of Christ.
V. Let us praise the Lord
R. And give him thanks.
V. May the divine assistance remain with us always
R. And with all our relatives and friends.
V. May all the departed through the mercy of God rest in peace.
R. Amen.

The proper conclusion of the feast or season or any other prayer may be used.

O Almighty God, I commend to you in this
spirit all the dead ... for the favors you have
bestowed upon me this day. To my God and this
my flesh ... and the powers of my body and soul.
... that you all turn their hearts after your own
and grow rich ... those other ways, or
which ... set ... heart toward them, ...
heavenly things, through Christ our Lord.
Amen.

V. Let us praise, O holy Mother of God.
R. That we may be made worthy of the promises
of Christ.

V. Let us praise the Lord
R. And give him thanks.
V. May the divine assistance remain with us al-
ways.
R. And with all our relatives and friends.
V. May all the departed through the mercy of God
rest in peace.
R. Amen.

the quiet conclusion of the concluding prayer or other
saying and

Proper Hymns, Readings and Conclusions

ADVENT

Hymn

Now hear the Voice! It thunders clear,
Denouncing every hidden wrong.
Away with all our dreaming now,
Christ comes from heaven with all his grace.

Now let the sluggish mind be stirred,
The mind long sick from filth of sin.
A newborn star had filled the night,
Made harmless all the hours of dark.

The Lamb is sent from height of heaven
Freely to cancel all our debt.
May tears and prayers of contrite hearts
Obtain our pardon and release.

And so when he returns with fire
And girdles all the world with dread,
He will not punish us for sin,
But shield us tenderly in love.

Give praise and honor, glory, power,
To God the Father and his Son,
To Holy Spirit, Paraclete,
Through time and all eternity. Amen.

Readings

Sunday. My brothers and sisters, the time has come for us to wake from sleep. For salvation is nearer to us now than when we first believed. (Romans 13:11)

Monday. In that day the remnant of Israel and the survivors of the house of Jacob will no longer lean upon him who smote them, but will lean upon the Lord, the Holy One of Israel, in truth. A remnant will return, the remnant of Jacob, to the mighty God. (Isaiah 10:20–21)

Tuesday. Behold, the days are coming, says the Lord, when I will raise up for David a righteous Branch, and he shall reign as king and deal wisely, and shall execute justice and righteousness in the land. (Jeremiah 23:5)

Wednesday. The haughty looks of man and woman shall be brought low, and the pride of them shall be humbled, and the Lord alone will be exalted in that day. (Isaiah 2:11)

Thursday. The ruler in Israel shall stand firm and shepherd his flock by the strength of the Lord, in the majestic name of the Lord, his God; and they shall remain, for now his greatness shall reach to the ends of the earth; he shall be peace. (Micah 5:3–5)

Friday. I know well the plans I have in mind for you, says the Lord, plans for your welfare; not for woe!—plans to give you a future full of hope.

When you look for me, you will find me, when
you seek me with all your heart. (Jeremiah 29:11–
13)

Saturday. On that day, the branch of the Lord will
be luster and glory, and the fruit of the earth will
be honor and splendor for the survivors of Israel.
(Isaiah 4:2)

Conclusion

V. The nations will revere your name, O Lord.

R. And the great ones of the earth will acknowledge your glory.

Lord, have mercy. Christ, have mercy. Lord, have
mercy.

Optional litanies: Appendix Three

Our Father, who art in heaven . . .

Let us pray.

(Pause for silent prayer.)

God our Father, you loved the world so much
you gave your only Son to free us from the ancient
power of sin and death. Help us who wait for his
coming and lead us to true freedom. Grant this
through Jesus Christ, your Son, our Lord. AMEN.

V. Pray for us, O holy Mother of God,

R. that we may be made worthy of the promises of Christ.

V. Let us praise the Lord

R. and give him thanks.

V. May the divine assistance remain with us always

R. and with all our relatives and friends.

V. May all the departed through the mercy of God rest in peace.

R. AMEN.

CHRISTMASTIME

Hymn

Christ, the all-redeeming,
The Father's only Child,
Beyond all telling, born of him
Before the world's began.

Father's light and splendor,
Timeless hope of all,
Heed the prayers your servants offer
Through the world this day.

Author of salvation,
Remember you were born—
you took the form of human flesh
From spotless Maiden's womb.

Again this day bears witness
With the returning year,
How you, the only hope we have,
Came from your Father's throne.

Each atom of creation,
The heavens, earth, and sea
Praise this day with joyful song,
The day when you were born.

We whom you redeemed,
The trophies of your blood,

Intone this never aging song,
Your birthday song of praise.

Glory, Lord, to you
Fruit of Maiden's womb,
With Father and the Holy Spirit,
Endless ages through. AMEN.

Readings

Sunday. The grace of God has appeared, offering salvation to all. It trains us to reject godless ways and worldly desires, and live temperately, justly, and devoutly in this age. (Titus 2:11–12)

Monday. Because you are God's chosen ones, holy and beloved, clothe yourselves with heartfelt mercy, faith, kindness, humility, meekness, and patience. Bear with one another; forgive whatever grievances you have against one another. Forgive as the Lord has forgiven you. (Colossians 3:12–13)

Tuesday. Here then is the message we have heard from him and announce to you: that God is light, in him there is no darkness. If we walk in light, as he is in the light, we have fellowship with one another, and the blood of his Son Jesus cleanses us from all sin. (1 John 1:5–7)

Wednesday. What great nation is there that has gods so close to it as the Lord, our God is to us whenever we call upon him? (Deuteronomy 4:7)

Thursday. It was I who stirred up one for the triumph of justice; all his ways I make level. He shall rebuild my city and let my exiles go free without price or ransom, says the Lord of hosts. (Isaiah 45:13)

Friday. You can depend on this as worthy of full acceptance, that Jesus Christ came into the world to save sinners. (1 Timothy 1:15)

Saturday. Shout for joy, O daughter Zion! Sing joyfully, O Israel! Be glad and exult with all your heart, O daughter Jerusalem! The Lord has removed the judgment against you, he has turned away your enemies. The King of Israel, the Lord, is in your midst, you have no further misfortune to fear. (Zephaniah 3:14–15)

Conclusion

V. The Lord has remembered his gracious promise, alleluia.
R. He has kept faith with his people Israel, alleluia.

Lord, have mercy. Christ, have mercy. Lord, have mercy.

Optional litanies: Appendix Three

Our Father, who art in heaven . . .

Let us pray.

(Pause for silent prayer.)

All-loving Father, you sent your Son Jesus Christ to bring the new light of salvation to the world. May he enlighten us with his radiance, he who lives and reigns with you and the Holy Spirit, our one God, for ever and ever. AMEN.

V. Pray for us, O holy Mother of God,

R. That we may be made worthy of the promises of Christ.

V. Let us praise the Lord

R. And give him thanks.

V. May the divine assistance remain with us always

R. And with all our relatives and friends.

V. May all the departed through the mercy of God rest in peace.

R. Amen.

LENT

Hymn

Harken, kind Creator,
To mingled prayers and tears
Through forty days and forty nights
Of holy lenten fast.

Your love has searched our hearts,
You know how frail our powers.
Grant us now, turned back to you,
Free pardon for our faults.

Our load of sin is great,
But spare, for we confess.
Give glory to your Name and heal
The sickness of our souls.

Grant that flesh be turned
By patient abstinence.
So chastened mind may learn to fast
From every taste of sin.

Then, Trinity most blessed,
One simple Godhead, grant
Your lenten gifts may bear full fruit
In every child of yours. AMEN.

Readings

Sunday. As your fellow workers we beg you not to receive the grace of God in vain. For he says: "In an acceptable time I have heard you; on a day of salvation I have helped you." Now is the acceptable time! Now is the day of salvation! (2 Corinthians 6:1–2)

Monday. Now, my brothers, we beg and exhort you in the Lord Jesus that, even as you learned from us how to conduct yourselves in a way pleasing to God—which you are indeed doing—so you must learn to make still greater progress. (1 Thessalonians 4:1)

Tuesday. Be imitators of God as his dear children. Follow the way of love, even as Christ loved you. He gave himself for us as an offering to God, a gift of pleasing fragrance. (Ephesians 5:1–2)

Wednesday. Yet even now, says the Lord, return to me with your whole heart, with fasting and weeping and mourning; rend your hearts, not your garments, and return to the Lord, your God. For gracious and merciful is he, slow to anger, rich in kindness, and relenting in punishment. (Joel 2:12–13)

Thursday. Therefore I will judge you, house of Israel, each one according to his ways, says the Lord God. Turn and be converted from all your crimes, that they may be no cause of guilt for you. Cast away from you all the crimes you have committed. And make for yourselves a new heart and a new spirit. Why should you die, O house of Israel? For I have no pleasure in the death of anyone who dies, says the Lord God. Return and live! (Ezekiel 18:30–32)

Friday. Seek the Lord while he may be found, call him while he is near. Let the scoundrel forsake his way and the wicked man his thoughts; let him turn to the Lord for mercy, to our God who is generous in forgiving. (Isaiah 55:6–7)

Saturday. Whoever is dear to me I reprove and chastise. Be earnest about it. Repent! Here I stand knocking at the door. If anyone hears me calling and opens the door, I will enter his house and have supper with him and he with me. (Revelation 3:19–20)

Conclusion

V. Create a clean heart in me, O God.
R. Renew in me a steadfast spirit.

Lord, have mercy. Christ, have mercy. Lord, have mercy.

Optional litanies: Appendix Three

Our Father, who art in heaven . . .

Let us pray.

(Pause for silent prayer.)

Father, you formed us from the clay of the earth and breathed into us the spirit of life, but we have turned from your face and sinned. In this time of repentance we call out for your mercy. Bring us back to you and to the life your Son won for us by his death on the cross for he lives and reigns with you in the Holy Spirit for ever and ever. AMEN.

V. Pray for us, O holy Mother of God,
R. That we may be made worthy of the promises of Christ.
V. Let us praise the Lord
R. And give him thanks.
V. May the divine assistance remain with us always
R. And with all our relatives and friends.
V. May all the departed through the mercy of God rest in peace.
R. AMEN.

HOLY WEEK

Hymn

Thirty years are now completed,
Time for living well fulfilled
He was born, he willed to suffer,
From conception sealed to death.
So the Lamb ascends the gibbet,
Climbs the altar of the cross.

Red and vinegar—the poison!
Spittle and the tearing nails!
Lance that pierces tender body,
Water flowing with the Blood!
Earth and ocean, stars, creation
Washed and cleansed by this pure flood!

Steadfast Cross, no peer beside you!
Noble tree that stands alone!
Never forest bore the equal,
Branches, flower, and priceless seed!
Sweet the wood, the nails so tender,
Bearing such a precious load.

Lofty Tree, bend low your branches,
Soften now your rigid breast.
Melt the hardness of your timber
That by nature's gift is yours.
Kindly stretch on bough now tender
Limbs and body of our King.

You alone deserved to carry
Ransom-price for fallen ones,
Worthy to prepare a harbor,
Pilot home the shipwrecked world,
Now anointed with the life blood
Of the immolated lamb.

Glory give to God, and honor,
Always, everywhere most high,
Father and the Son together
With the glorious Paraclete!
Theirs be power and theirs be worship
Now through all eternity. AMEN.

Readings

Sunday. Continually we carry about in our bodies the dying of Jesus, so that in our bodies the life of Jesus may also be revealed. While we live we are constantly being delivered to death for Jesus' sake, so that the life of Jesus may be revealed in our mortal flesh. Death is at work in us, but life in you. (2 Corinthians 4:10–12)

Monday. You people say, "Our crimes and our sins weigh us down; we are rotting away because of them. How can we survive?" As I live, says the Lord God, I swear I take no pleasure in the death of the wicked but rather in the wicked's conversion that he may live. (Ezekiel 33:10–11)

Tuesday. God wants all to be saved and come to know the truth. And the truth is this: "God is one. One also is the mediator between God and us, the Man Christ Jesus, who gave himself as a ransom for all." (1 Timothy 2:4–6)

Wednesday. The message of the cross is complete absurdity to those who are headed for ruin, but to us who are experiencing salvation it is the power of God. Scripture says, "I will destroy the wisdom of the wise, and thwart the cleverness of the clever." (1 Corinthians 1:18–19)

Thursday. Since we have a great high priest who has passed through the heavens, Jesus, the Son of God, let us hold fast to our profession of faith. For we do not have a high priest who is unable to sympathize with our weakness, but one who was tempted in every way that we are, yet never sinned. (Hebrews 4:14–15)

Friday. He grew like a sapling before the Lord, like a shoot from the parched earth; there was in him no stately bearing to make us look at him, no appearance that would attract us to him. He was spurned and avoided by all, a man of suffering, accustomed to infirmity, one of those from whom all hide their faces, spurned, and we held him in no esteem. (Isaiah 53:2–3)

Saturday. If we say, "We are free of the guilt of sin," we deceive ourselves; the truth is not to be found in us. But if we acknowledge our sins, he who is just can be trusted to forgive our sins and cleanse us from every wrong. (1 John 1:8–9)

Conclusion

V. He freely gave himself up in sacrifice.
R. He said no word in his own defense.

Lord, have mercy. Christ, have mercy. Lord, have mercy.

Optional litanies: Appendix Three

Our Father, who art in heaven . . .

Let us pray.

140

(Pause for silent prayer.)

Father, may we receive your forgiveness and mercy as we relive the passion and death of our Lord, who lives and reigns now with you and the Holy Spirit, our one God, for ever and ever. AMEN.

V. Pray for us, O holy Mother of God,
R. That we may be made worthy of the promises of Christ.
V. Let us praise the Lord
R. And give him thanks.
V. May the divine assistance remain with us always
R. And with all our relatives and friends.
V. May all the departed through the mercy of God rest in peace.
R. AMEN.

EASTERTIME

Hymn

Called to the supper of the Lamb,
Clothed in purest light,
The Red Sea's waters far behind,
We sing of Christ our King.

We live, we live to God
When, with his crimson Blood,
We taste that holiest Flesh of his
Burnt on the altar-cross.

Saved that Paschal evening
From angel's stroke of death,
We now are snatched from Pharaoh's power,
Freed from cruelest yoke.

Christ, our Paschal Lamb,
Was slain to give us life;
Unleavened bread of purest flour,
His flesh was offered up.

That truly worthy victim
Burst the bonds of hell,
Redeemed the captive folk of God,
Gave back the gift of life.

He rent the rock-bound tomb,
Came victor from the depths,

142

Enchained the tyrant, cast him down,
Flung wide the gates of heaven.

In Paschal joy we pray
Our God, creating all,
Defend your people now redeemed
From all assault of death.

Glory, Lord, to you,
Risen from the tomb,
With Father and the Holy Spirit,
Endless ages through. AMEN.

Readings

Sunday. I handed on to you first of all what I myself received that Christ died for our sins in accordance with the Scriptures; that he was buried and, in accordance with the Scriptures, rose on the third day; that he was seen by Cephas then by the Twelve. (1 Corinthians 15:3–5)

Monday. When I caught sight of him I fell down at his feet as though dead. He touched me with his right hand and said: "There is nothing to fear. I am the First and the Last and the One who lives. Once I was dead but now I live—for ever and ever. I hold the keys of death and the nether world." (Revelation 1:17–18)

Tuesday. Since you have been raised up in company with Christ, set your heart on what pertains to higher realms where Christ is seated at God's right hand. Be intent on things above rather than on things of earth. (Colossians 3:1–2)

Wednesday. Our faith will be credited to us also if we believe in him who raised Jesus our Lord from the dead, the Jesus who was handed over to death for our sins and raised up for our justification. (Romans 4:24–25)

Thursday. It was in one Spirit that all of us, whether Jew or Greek, slave or free, were baptized into one body. All of us have been given to drink of the same Spirit. (1 Corinthians 12–13)

Friday. This is the Jesus God has raised up, and we

are his witnesses. Exalted at God's right hand, he first received the promised Holy Spirit from the Father, then poured this Spirit out on us. This is what you now see and hear. (Acts 2:32–33)

Saturday. For if, when we were God's enemies, we were reconciled to him by the death of his Son, it is all the more certain that we who have been reconciled will be saved by his life. Not only that; we go so far as to make God our boast through our Lord Jesus Christ, through whom we have now received reconciliation. (Romans 5:10–11)

Conclusion

V. The Lord is risen, alleluia!
R. He has appeared to Simon, alleluia!

Lord, have mercy. Christ, have mercy. Lord, have mercy.

Optional litanies: Appendix Three

Our Father, who art in heaven . . .

Let us pray.

(Pause for silent prayer.)

Father, by the love of your Spirit, may we who have experienced the grace of the Lord's resurrection rise to a newness of life in joy. Grant this through Christ our risen Lord. AMEN.

V. Pray for us, O holy Mother of God,
R. That we may be made worthy of the promises of Christ.
V. Let us praise the Lord
R. And give him thanks.
V. May the divine assistance remain with us always
R. And with all our relatives and friends.
V. May all the departed through the mercy of God rest in peace.
R. AMEN.

PENTECOST

Hymn

The time of year returns
With wealth of heavenly joy,
When first the Paraclete came
Upon the friends of Christ.

He came in form of tongues
Alive with light and fire,
To give them power and grace in word,
And fervor in their love.

They speak the tongues of all;
The gathered nations fear;
They think that those the Spirit fills
Are drunk with earthly wine.

With Easter time fulfilled,
All bears a mystic sense;
Through sacred numbering of days
The law would cancel sin.

To you, most loving God,
Humbled in heart we pray;
Grant us from heaven that wealth of gifts
The Holy Spirit brings.

Of old you graced the souls
Who gave themselves to you;

147

Give pardon now for all our sin
And peace within our time.

Glory to God the Father
To the Son who conquered death,
And glory to the Paraclete
Now and eternally. AMEN.

Readings

Sunday. When the day of Pentecost arrived, the disciples were all together in one place. Suddenly from heaven came a sound like a violent wind blowing and it filled the whole house where they were sitting. (Acts 2:1–2)

Monday. At the sound a great crowd gathered and each one was bewildered to hear his own language being spoken. (Acts 2:6)

Tuesday. Jews by birth and by conversion, Cretans and Arabians, each of us has heard them telling in our own language of the wonderful works of God. (Acts 2:11)

Wednesday. How deep the mine of God's wisdom and knowledge! How inscrutable his judgments, how unsearchable his ways! (Romans 11:33)

Thursday. May the grace of our Lord Jesus Christ, and the love of God, and the fellowship of the Holy Spirit be with you all. (2 Corinthians 13:13)

Friday. There are three who give testimony in heaven, the Father, the Word, and the Holy Spirit, three who are yet one. (1 John 5:7)

Saturday. Just as in one body we have many different organs, yet not all the organs have the same function, even so we, though many in number, comprise one body in Christ, with each individual serving to complement the others in Christ Jesus our Lord. (Romans 12:4–5)

Conclusion

V. The apostles spoke in various languages, alleluia!

R. Telling of the wonderful works of God, alleluia!

Lord, have mercy. Christ, have mercy. Lord, have mercy.

Optional litanies: Appendix Three

Our Father, who art in heaven . . .

Let us pray.

(Pause for silent prayer.)

Father, you opened the understanding of the faithful by the light of the Holy Spirit whom you sent into our hearts, grant us by the same Spirit to relish what is right, and to find our joy at all times in the comfort which he brings. We ask this through our Lord Jesus Christ, your Son, who lives and reigns with you and the Holy Spirit now and forever. AMEN.

V. Pray for us, O holy Mother of God,

R. That we may be made worthy of the promises of Christ.

V. Let us praise the Lord

R. And give him thanks.

V. May the divine assistance remain with us always
R. And with all our relatives and friends.
V. May all the departed through the mercy of God rest in peace.
R. AMEN.

FEASTS OF THE BLESSED VIRGIN MARY

Hymn

Star of this dark ocean,
Mother of our God,
Yet a maiden always,
Gateway to the sky.

Seizing on that "Ave,"
Gabriel's gift from God,
Give us peace from heaven,
Joy for Eve at last.

Break the prisoner's bondage,
Blind eyes flood with light;
Drive all evil from us,
Plead for all our good.

Prove yourself a mother,
Give to Christ our prayers;
He deigned to be your infant,
Born to win our souls.

Maiden with no equal,
Meekest of the meek,
Hold us back from sinning,
Mold us meek and chaste.

Pure be each day's living,
Each day's journey safe;
When beholding Jesus,
endless joy be ours.

Praise to God the Father,
Praise to Christ most high,
Praise to Holy Spirit,
One worship to all Three. AMEN.

Reading

When the designated time had come, God sent forth his Son born of a woman, born under the law, to deliver from the law those who were subjected to it, so that we might receive our status as adopted children.

Conclusion

V. The Lord has chosen her.
R. She belongs to him.

Lord, have mercy. Christ, have mercy. Lord, have mercy.

Optional litanies: Appendix Three

Our Father, who art in heaven . . .

Let us pray.

(Pause for silent prayer.)

Father, all-loving and eternal, in the Blessed Virgin Mary's heart you prepared a dwelling worthy of your Son. In your mercy grant that we who devoutly honor the blessed Virgin may be able to live according to your desires. We ask this through

our Lord Jesus, who lives and reigns with you and
the Holy Spirit, our one God, for ever and ever.
AMEN.

V. Pray for us, O holy Mother of God,
R. That we may be made worthy of the promises
of Christ.
V. Let us praise the Lord
R. And give him thanks.
V. May the divine assistance remain with us al-
ways
R. And with all our relatives and friends.
V. May all the departed through the mercy of God
rest in peace.
R. AMEN.

FEASTS OF APOSTLES

Hymn

Let praise sweep through the heavens,
Joy thunder from the earth,
As pilgrim Church invites us all
To praise the chosen twelve.

O lights that shatter darkness,
Judges of the world,
To you our contrite hearts send up
Their beggar cry for help.

Heaven's gate swings open
Or shuts, as you decree.
Speak, command the chains of sin
To fall from prisoner souls.

Christ gave you apostles
Power to cure disease.
Our hearts are sin-sick, ease their hurt
With virtue's healing strength.

That when Christ comes in judgment,
And brings time to an end,
Then God may take us all to himself
To share with us his joy.

Glory to God the Father,
To Christ, his only Son,
Glory to Spirit Paraclete
Now and beyond all time. AMEN.

Reading

My friends, you are now no longer guests and aliens, for you are fellow citizens with the saints, and members of God's household. Apostles and prophets are the foundation on which you were built and the chief cornerstone is Jesus Christ himself. (Ephesians 2:19–20)

Conclusion

V. What honor your friends receive, O God!
R. What sovereign power is theirs!

Lord, have mercy. Christ, have mercy. Lord, have mercy.

Optional litanies: Appendix Three

Our Father, who art in heaven . . .

Let us pray.

(Pause for silent prayer.)

Father, you have made your Church holy by the teaching of your apostles. Grant that we might follow in all things the witness of those from whom

we have received th faith. We ask this through our
Lord Jesus, in the Holy Spirit. AMEN.

V. Pray for us, O holy Mother of God,
R. That we may be made worthy of the promises
of Christ.
V. Let us praise the Lord
R. And give him thanks.
V. May the divine assistance remain with us al-
ways
R. And with all our relatives and friends.
V. May all the departed through the mercy of God
rest in peace.
R. AMEN.

Hymn

Martyr of God, who followed
The Father's only Son,
Defeated every foe, received
The victor's palm of life.

May souls befouled by guilt
Find cleansing through your prayer.
Be buckler shielding hearts, dispel
Life's boredom, sin's disease.

Death brought soul's release,
Freedom to be with Christ.
Break with Christ's strong love, O break
These chains that choke my heart!

Glory to God the Father,
To Christ, his only Son,
Glory to Spirit Paraclete
Now and beyond all time. AMEN.

Reading

Happy those who undergo trial. When they have proved their worth, they will receive the crown of life promised by God to those who love him. (James 1:12)

Conclusion

V. The just will grow like the lily.
R. They will flourish for ever in the presence of the Lord.

Lord, have mercy. Christ, have mercy. Lord, have mercy.

Optional litanies: Appendix Three

Our Father, who art in heaven . . .

Let us pray.

(Pause for silent prayer.)

Father, all-loving and eternal God, you gave your martyr that love which seeks not its own interests. Tear from our hearts the thorns of inordinate self-love, the root of every evil, so that we may love ourselves as we truly should, and in that love serve all our sisters and brothers. We ask this through the great martyr, your Son, our Lord Jesus Christ. AMEN.

V. Pray for us, O holy Mother of God,
R. That we may be made worthy of the promises of Christ.
V. Let us praise the Lord
R. And give him thanks.
V. May the divine assistance remain with us always
R. And with all our relatives and friends.
V. May all the departed through the mercy of God rest in peace.
R. AMEN.

FEASTS OF OTHER SAINTS

Hymn

Jesus the only crown,
The primal word of truth,
Timeless reward for time's good faith
You give your servants now.

Grant us suppliant here,
Through this new Christ in grace,
Remission for our crime and sin,
And freedom from our bonds.

With the returning year
The day has dawned again
When this your saint laid down the flesh
And strongly seized on heaven.

Poor pleasures of the earth
With rich estates and lands
Are counted dung; we claim with joy
The kingdom of our God.

Always confessing you,
Christ King so good,
We bravely trod the enemy down,
His pride and all his train.

In faith and virtue strong,
Each day confessing you,
And fasting here, this saint now tastes
The Eucharist of heaven.

We beg you, God of love,
With prostrate souls in prayer,
Through this saint's life of fruitful grace,
Full pardon of our sins.

Glory, Lord and Father,
glory, only Son,
One glory to the Holy Spirit
Endless ages through. AMEN.

Reading

Happy the one found unblemished, who has not gone after gold, nor put trust in money or store of riches. Show us such a person, that we may praise this saint; for such a one has done wonderful things during life.

Conclusion

V. The lips of the just speak wisdom.
R. The righteous one proclaims true judgment.

Lord, have mercy. Christ, have mercy. Lord, have mercy.

Optional litanies: Appendix Three

Our Father, who art in heaven . . .

Let us pray.

(Pause for silent prayer.)

Father of love and mercy, your will to instruct your pilgrim people is as unfailing as your will to come to our assistance. Through the intercession of your servant whom we honor this day may we obtain both the understanding we need to know your will and the grace to carry it out faithfully. We ask this, Father, through your Son, Jesus Christ, our Lord. Amen.

V. Pray for us, O holy Mother of God,
R. That we may be made worthy of the promises of Christ.
V. Let us praise the Lord
R. And give him thanks.
V. May the divine assistance remain with us always
R. And with all our relatives and friends.
V. May all the departed through the mercy of God rest in peace.
R. Amen.

The Office of Readings

Opening

V. O Lord, open my eyes and my ears

R. And my whole being shall praise your holy name.

Glory be to the Father and to the Son and to the Holy Spirit,

As it was in the beginning, is now and ever shall be. AMEN.

Hymn

Come, Holy Spirit, Come!
And from your celestial home
shed a ray of light divine.

Come, Father of the poor!
Come, Source of all our store!
Come, within our bosoms shine!

You, of comforters the best;
you, the soul's most welcome guest;
sweet refreshment here below;

In our labor, rest most sweet;
grateful coolness in the heat;
solace in the midst of woe.

O most blessed Light divine,
shine within these hearts of thine,
and our inmost being fill!

Where you are not, man has naught,
nothing good in deed or thought,
nothing free from taint of ill.

Heal our wounds, our strength renew;
on our dryness, pour your dew;
wash the stains of guilt away.

Bend the stubborn heart and will;
melt the frozen, warm the chill;
guide the steps that go astray.

On the faithful, who adore
and confess you, evermore
in your sev'nfold gift descend.

Give them virtue's sure reward;
give them your salvation, Lord;
give them joys that never end. AMEN.

The proper hymn of the feast or season or any other hymn may be used.

Psalms

Psalm 78 [77]

Listen to this law, my people,
pay attention to what I say;
I am going to speak to you in parables
and expound the mysteries of our past.

What we have heard and known for ourselves,
and what our ancestors have told us,
must not be withheld from their descendants,
but be handed on by us to the next generation;

that is: the titles of Yahweh, his power
and the miracles he has done.
When he issued the decrees for Jacob
and instituted a law in Israel,

he gave our ancestors strict orders
to teach it to their children;
the next generation was to learn it,
the children still to be born,

and these in their turn were to tell their own
    children
so that they, too, would put their confidence in
    God,
never forgetting God's achievements,
and always keeping his commandments.

Praise to the Father almighty,
to his Son, Jesus Christ, our Lord,
to their Spirit who dwells in our hearts,
both now and forever. AMEN.

First Reading

The first reading is taken from the Sacred Scriptures. You may use any passage you wish.

Some suggestions:

1. Use the passages assigned for the day's Mass.

2. *Lectio continuata*—continuous reading; i.e., read the Bible through, a chapter or two each day.

3. You might like to follow the traditional order for the *lectio continuata:*

From the first Sunday of Advent to Circumcision: Isaiah

From Circumcision to Ash Wednesday: Epistles of St. Paul

From Ash Wednesday to Holy Week: Genesis through Judges

Holy Week: Jeremiah and Baruch

From Easter to Pentecost: Acts of the Apostles, Revelation, the other Epistles

From Pentecost to August: Samuel, Kings, Chronicles, Ezra

August: The Wisdom books

September: Job, Tobias, Judith, Esther

October: Maccabees
November: Ezekiel, Daniel, the Minor Prophets

4. You may wish to use the method of Sacred Reading to be found in the First Appendix.

(Pause for silent reflection.)

Responsorial Psalm

Psalm 119 [118]

Yahweh, may my cry approach your presence;
    let your word endow me with perception!
May my entreaty reach your presence;
    rescue me as you have promised.
May my lips proclaim your praise,
    since you teach me your statutes.
May my tongue recite your promise,
    since all your commandments are righteous.
May your hand be there to help me,
    since I have chosen your precepts.
I long for you, Yahweh, my savior,
    your law is my delight.
Long may my soul live to praise you,
    long be your rulings my help!
I am wandering like a lost sheep:
    come and look for your servant.

No, I have never forgotten your commandments.

Praise to the Father almighty,
   to his Son, Jesus Christ, our Lord,
to their Spirit who dwells in our hearts,
   both now and forever. AMEN.

Second Reading

The second reading may be taken from any book offering edification. The writings of the Fathers and Mothers of the Church and those of the saints are recommended, especially their commentaries on the Sacred Scriptures. Anthologies such as *Through the Year with the Saints* are most convenient and give readings appropriate to the particular day.

You may certainly feel free to choose a work of some modern author, such as Thomas Merton, and read a portion of it each day.

(Pause for silent reflection.)

Conclusion

V. May your Word give us light.
R. May it enlighten our path to eternal life.

Lord, have mercy. Christ, have mercy. Lord, have mercy.

Optional litanies: Appendix Three

Our Father, who art in heaven . . . .

Let us pray.

(Pause for silent prayer.)

Father, we thank you for the words of wisdom
which you have imparted to us this day. May we
not only understand them but put them into practice. This we ask through your Son, Jesus Christ,
our Lord, who lives and reigns with you and the
Holy Spirit, our one God, now and forever. AMEN.

V. Pray for us, O holy Mother of God,
R. That we may be made worthy of the promises
of Christ.
V. Let us praise the Lord
R. And give him thanks.
V. May the divine assistance remain with us al-
ways
R. And with all our relatives and friends.
V. May all the departed through the mercy of God
rest in peace.
R. AMEN.

Compline

Opening

V. O God, come to our assistance.
R. O Lord, make haste to help us.
  Glory be to the Father and to the Son and to the
  Holy Spirit,
  as it was in the beginning is now and ever shall
  be, world without end. AMEN.

Psalms

Psalm 4

God, guardian of my rights, you answer when I
call,
  when I am in trouble, you come to my relief;
  now be good to me and hear my prayer.

You men, why shut your hearts so long,
loving delusions, chasing after lies?

Know this, Yahweh works wonders for those he
   loves,
Yahweh hears me when I call to him.

   Tremble: give up sinning,
spend your night in quiet meditation.
Offer sacrifice in a right spirit, and trust Yahweh.

"Who will give us sight of happiness?" many say.
Show us the light of your face, turned toward us!

Yahweh, you have given more joy to my heart
than others ever knew for all their corn and wine.

In peace I lie down, and fall asleep at once,
since you alone, Yahweh, make me rest secure.

Praise to the Father almighty,
   to his Son, Jesus Christ, our Lord,
to their Spirit who dwells in our hearts,
   both now and forever. AMEN.

Psalm 91 [90]

If you live in the shelter of God
and make your home in the shadow of the Lord,
you can say to Yahweh, "My refuge, my fortress,
my God in whom I trust!"

He rescues from the snares
of fowlers hoping to destroy you;

176

he covers you with his feathers,
and you find shelter underneath his wings.

You need not fear the terrors of the night,
the arrow that flies in the daytime,
the plague that stalks in the dark,
the scourge that wreaks havoc in the broad
    daylight.

Though a thousand fall at your side,
ten thousand at your right hand,
you yourself remain unscathed,
with his faithfulness for shield and buckler.

You have only to look around
to see how the wicked are repaid,
you can say, "Yahweh, my refuge,"
and make God your fortress.

No disaster can overtake you,
no plague come near your tent:
he will put you in his angels' charge
to guide you wherever you go.

They will support you on their hands
lest you hurt your foot against the stone;
you will tread on lion and adder,
trample on savage lions and dragons.

"I rescue all who cling to me,
I protect whoever knows my name,
I answer everyone who invokes me,
I am with them when they are in trouble;

I bring them safety and honor.
I give them life, long and full,
and show them how I can save."

Praise to the Father almighty,
    to his Son, Jesus Christ, our Lord,
to their Spirit who dwells in our hearts,
    both now and forever. AMEN.

Psalm 134 [133]

Come bless Yahweh, all you who serve,
serving in the house of Yahweh,
in the courts of our God.
Stretch out your hands toward the sanctuary,
bless Yahweh night after night!

May Yahweh bless you from Zion,
he who made heaven and earth!

Praise to the Father almighty,
    to his Son, Jesus Christ, our Lord,
to their Spirit who dwells in our hearts,
    both now and forever. AMEN.

Reading

You are in our midst, O Lord, and your name we bear. Do not forsake us, O Lord our God. (Jeremiah 14:9)

R. Thanks be to God.

(Pause for silent reflection.)

Conclusion

V. Keep us, Lord, as the apple of your eye.
R. Hide us in the shelter of your wings.

The Canticle of Simeon
The Nunc dimittis
Luke 2:29–32

Now, Master, you can let your servant go in
     peace,
just as you promised;
because my eyes have seen the salvation
which you have prepared for all the nations to
     see,
a light to enlighten the pagans
and the glory of your people Israel.

Praise to the Father almighty,
    to his Son, Jesus Christ, our Lord,
to their Spirit who dwells in our hearts,
    both now and forever. AMEN.

Lord, have mercy. Christ, have mercy. Lord, have mercy.

Optional litanies: Appendix Three

Our Father, who art in heaven . . .

Let us pray.

(Pause for silent prayer.)

Lord, visit this house and all who call it home and protect us from all evil. May your holy angels dwell here and keep us in peace and may your blessing be upon us always. We ask this through Jesus, your Son, who lives and reigns with you and the Holy Spirit, our one God, now and forever. AMEN.

BLESSING: May the Lord all powerful and merciful, Father, Son and Holy Spirit, bless and watch over us. AMEN.

Hail, Holy Queen

Salve, Regina

Hail, holy Queen, Mother of Mercy, our life, our sweetness, and our hope. To you do we cry, poor banished children of Eve. To you do we send up our sighs, mourning, and weeping in this vale of tears. Turn, then, O most gracious Advocate, your eyes of mercy toward us. And after this our exile, show unto us the blessed Fruit of your womb, Jesus. O clement, O loving, O sweet Virgin Mary.

Appendices

One: Sacred Reading

It is well to keep the Sacred Scriptures enthroned in our homes in a place of honor as a real presence of the Word in our midst.

1. Take the Sacred Text with reverence and call upon the Holy Spirit.

2. For ten minutes (or longer, if you are so drawn), listen to the Lord speaking to you through the Text, and respond to him.

3. At the end of the time, choose a word or phrase (perhaps one will have been "given" to you) to take with you, and thank the Lord for being with you and speaking to you.

For Scriptural Prayer any part of the Bible may be chosen. Some like to use the readings assigned by the Lectionary for reading at that particular day's Mass. Others like to follow the Bible through, taking each day that portion which is sufficient to nourish them. Others like to open the Bible randomly after calling upon the Holy Spirit to guide them—this is fine so long as there is no superstition attached to it.

Usually we do well to begin with the New Testament, especially the Gospels. Saint John's chapters on the Last Supper are especially deep and meaningful: John 13–17. Matthew's reporting of the Sermon on the Mount is another favorite that is most fruitful: Matthew 5–7. The Psalms are another favorite book of the Bible. A combination, beginning with some Gospel reading and then concluding with a single Psalm, might be very good.

Before using the Epistles for Scriptural Prayer it might be well to read them as letters in the context of the Acts of the Apostles. Read the Acts through, and as you encounter Paul's evangelization of the particular churches, stop and read the Epistle(s) to the Church. Read it as a letter, read it right through, getting the whole sense of the Epistle as a letter from your revered teacher.

Whatever order you choose, do not be overly concerned about it, but rather be concerned simply to hear the Lord speaking to you through his inspired Word, speaking to your heart.

Two: Centering Prayer

"Centering Prayer" is a modern name, deriving from Thomas Merton, for an ancient method of prayer coming from the same source as the Jesus Prayer. It was brought to the West by Saint John Cassian in the early fifth century. It presupposes

Gospel Prayer and other forms of prayer have brought us to the point where we are desirous in faith simply to be with God in love. The method is very simple.

Sit comfortably in a chair that will give your back good support, and gently close your eyes. It is well to choose a place where you will not be disturbed by any sudden intrusion. A quiet place is helpful, though not necessary.

1. At the beginning of the Prayer take a minute or two to quiet down and then turn in faith and love to God dwelling in the depths of your being.

2. After resting for a bit in the center in faith-filled love, take up a single, simple word that expresses your being to God and let this word be gently present, directing your presence to the Presence, to God in you.

3. Whenever in the course of the Prayer you become aware of anything else, simply return to the Presence by gently using your prayer word.

4. At the end of your Prayer (we recommend a twenty-minute period, if possible), take a couple of minutes to come out of the Prayer, slowly praying the "Our Father" or some other favorite prayer.

Further teaching on this method of prayer may be found in the Image paperbacks *Daily We Touch Him* and *Centering Prayer*.

Three: Optional Litanies

These are meant to be merely suggestive. We do well to formulate our own petitions according to our own dispositions and needs.

Lord of all, you came into the world, that your name might be glorified in every place, strengthen the witness of your Church among the nations. *Lord, have mercy.*

Christ, herald of reconciliation, victor of the cross, free us from empty fear and hopelessness. *Christ, have mercy.*

Lord, fulfill your promise to those who already sleep in your peace, grant them a blessed resurrection. *Lord, have mercy.*

Lord, our strength, you called your faithful ones to your truth, mercifully grant them faith and perseverance. *Lord, have mercy.*

Have mercy on the needy, Lord, provide food for the hungry. *Christ, have mercy.*

Come to the aid of our departed sisters and brothers, whom you have redeemed with your blood, make them worthy to enter your wedding feast. *Lord, have mercy.*

Remember your Church, Lord, keep it from every evil and let it grow to the fullness of your love. *Lord, have mercy.*

Grant prosperity to our neighbors, give them life and happiness for ever. *Christ, have mercy.*

Open wide your compassion to those who have died today, and in your mercy receive them into your kingdom. *Lord, have mercy.*

King of the universe, Lord of every nation, guide and protect our people in justice and peace. *Lord, have mercy.*

Be present, Christ, to those who govern us, grant them wisdom and compassion in all that they do. *Christ, have mercy.*

To those who have laid down their lives for the nation that they loved, grant the blessings of your unending peace. *Lord, have mercy.*

Lord, you gave Mary to us as our mother. Through her intercession grant strength to the weak, comfort to the sorrowing, pardon to sinners. *Lord, have mercy.*

You made Mary open to your word and faithful as your disciple. Through her intercession make us servants and true followers. *Christ, have mercy.*

You crowned Mary queen of heaven, may all the dead rejoice in your kingdom with the saints forever. *Lord, have mercy.*

Lord, we are called your disciples and such we truly are; may the Church proclaim you to all men and women throughout the world. *Lord, have mercy.*

You have called us to walk before you and to please you in all we do, let us abound in doing good works. *Christ, have mercy.*

Bid the saints of heaven, your chosen friends,

to come to welcome our brothers and sisters who have died this day. *Lord, have mercy.*

Jesus, whose heart when pierced by a lance poured forth blood and water and gave birth to your spouse the Church, cleanse and sanctify us. *Lord, have mercy.*

Jesus, our life and resurrection, you refresh the burdened and give rest to the weary, draw all sinners to yourself. *Christ, have mercy.*

Jesus, because you loved us with so great a love, you were obedient even to death on the cross, raise up again all who sleep in your peace. *Lord, have mercy.*

Christ, bread of heaven, you form one body out of all who partake of one bread, refresh all who believe in you with harmony and peace. *Lord, have mercy.*

Christ, through your bread you offer the remedy for mortality and the pledge of future resurrection, restore health to the sick and living hope to sinners. *Christ, have mercy.*

Christ, our king who is to come, you commanded that the mysteries which proclaim your death be celebrated until you return, grant that all who die in you may share in your resurrection. *Lord, have mercy.*

Laus tibi, Christi.

OTHER IMAGE BOOKS

OTHER IMAGE BOOKS

CROSSWAYS – Fulton J. Sheen

A CRY FOR MERCY – Henri J. M. Nouwen

DAILY WE FOLLOW HIM – M. Basil Pennington, O.C.S.O.

DAILY WE TOUCH HIM – M. Basil Pennington, O.C.S.O.

DARK NIGHT OF THE SOUL – St. John of the Cross. Ed. and
  trans. by E. Allison Peers

DOORS TO THE SACRED – Joseph Martos

ESSENTIAL CATHOLICISM – Thomas Bokenkotter

ETERNAL LIFE? – Hans Küng

FREE TO BE HUMAN – Eugene Kennedy

GENESEE DIARY – Henri J. M. Nouwen

GOD LOVE YOU – Fulton J. Sheen

THE HEALING POWER OF AFFIRMATION – Fr. Ralph A. DiOrio

HE LEADETH ME – Walter J. Ciszek, S.J., with Daniel Flaherty,
  S.J.

A HISTORY OF PHILOSOPHY – Frederick Copleston, S.J.

Complete and unabridged in three Image Books

Book One: Volume I – Greece and Rome
          Volume II – Medieval Philosophy (Augustine to
            Duns Scotus)
          Volume III – Late Medieval and Renaissance Phi-
            losophy (Ockham to Suarez)

Book Two: Volume IV – Modern Philosophy (Descartes to
            Leibniz)
          Volume V – Modern Philosophy (The British Phi-
            losophers Hobbes to Hume)
          Volume VI – Modern Philosophy (The French
            Enlightenment to Kant)

Book Three: Volume VII – Modern Philosophy (Fichte to
              Nietzsche)
            Volume VIII – Modern Philosophy (Bentham to
              Russell)
            Volume IX – Modern Philosophy (Maine de
              Biran to Sarte)

A 88-2

OTHER IMAGE BOOKS

OTHER IMAGE BOOKS

A 88-4